Debbie Myers
524 Ho
Clarksville
283-3290
Dec 14, 1990

SAFE AND SOUND

SAFE AND SOUND

A PARENTS' GUIDE TO THE CARE OF CHILDREN HOME ALONE

TRUDY K. DANA

McGRAW-HILL BOOK COMPANY

New York   St. Louis   San Francisco   Bogotá
Hamburg   Madrid   Mexico   Milan   Montreal
Panama   Paris   São Paulo   Tokyo   Toronto

1 2 3 4 5 6 7 8 9 F G R F G R 8 9 2 1 0 9 8

ISBN 0-07-015283-7

LIBRARY OF CONGRESS CATALOGING-IN-PUBLICATION DATA

Dana, Trudy.
  Safe and sound.

    1. Safety education—United States. 2. Children's
accidents—Prevention—Study and teaching—United
States. 3. Child molesting—Prevention—Study and
teaching—United States. I. Title.
HQ770.7.D36 1988   649   87-3112
ISBN 0-07-015283-7

Illustrations by Mark Cretin

To my parents, who taught me I could do almost anything I wanted, and especially to my mother, who is always willing to help me achieve those dreams. To my husband, whose love and support helped make this book possible. And to my daughters, who have made being a mother worthwhile and fulfilling.

CONTENTS

Chapter 6: KIDS IN THE KITCHEN   **59**

ACKNOWLEDGMENTS

I want to thank the following people who so generously shared with me their expertise and experience to make this book a reality: Tom Kempton, Anchorage Fire Department; Donald Smith, Seattle Lutheran Counseling Network; Captain Allen Dillon, Lynwood Fire Department; Roger Dalzell and Robin Hickok, Edmonds Police Department; Dale Tallman, Seattle Police Department; Brian McIntosh, Edmonds Parks and Recreation; Margaret Martin, Edmonds Library; Jim Smith, Edmonds Animal Control; Asst. Chief Ron Schirman, Edmonds Fire Department; Dr. Ray Cardwell, Dr. Christine Caldwell, and Nurse Maryanne Straight, Edmonds Children's Clinic; Dr. Michael Rothenberg, Seattle Children's Hospital and Medical Center; Dr. James Seather; Psychologist Marilyn Grey; Nita Smith, Burien Boys Club; Mike Bocianowski, The Christensen Firm; Diane Gibbons, University of Hawaii; Greg Cobb, Stevens Hospital; Tom Snyder, Edmonds Postmaster; Kathy Harte, ARCO Alaska; Sherry Robb and Bart Andrews, Andrews and Robb Agents; and PJ Haduch and Elisabeth Jakab, my editors at McGraw-Hill.

I also want to thank the following friends and family members for the encouragement and support they so willingly gave: My sister, Gail Marshall; my parents-in-law, Christina and Ellis Dana; Dr. Berre and Anne D. Robinson; Chris and Rich McCroskey; Lydia and Dave Whitney; Julie Zwink; Tina Strausz; Judy Kawabori; Linda Meyer; Joy and Hank Smith; Pastors Jerry Myatt and Gary Stabbert; Bev Fosmark; Kathleen Angell; Shirley Margeson; Helena Strand and Alyce Wiggins; and most of all, I want to thank my mother, Phyllis E. Kempton, for the many, many hours she spent advising and editing.

INTRODUCTION

Keeping children safe and sound in today's world is a confusing and complex paradox for parents. We want to keep our children close, but at the same time encourage them to try their own wings. We want to protect and nurture them, yet we realize they must start to become independent, too. To compound our dilemma, most of us lead such busy lives that we have only a limited amount of time to spend with our youngsters.

As caring and concerned parents, we cannot simply declare our youngsters independent, then sit back and hope for the best. The process of letting go of our children should be gradual and progressive. We must prepare our youngsters by teaching them the skills they need to be safe and sound in this less than perfect world. That's what this book is all about. It is written so that parents can teach children the vital things they must learn in order to take care of themselves. Once our children master these skills, they are better able to face the world with competence and confidence.

I first became interested in writing a book like this in the late 1970s when I was teaching outdoor wilderness survival to youngsters in Seattle, Washington. I noticed that students in those classes asked questions that had nothing whatsoever to do with wilderness survival. It was evident that an overwhelming number of children had a much more urgent need for indoor survival skills than for outdoor training. These were the youngsters who were home alone taking care of themselves. When I did some research on this problem, my findings were sobering.

Here are some shocking statistics: In the United States alone, it is estimated that one-third of all elementary school children care for themselves regularly while their parents are at work. These children are home alone every day—before school, after school, or sometimes both. Often the youngsters must care for themselves the entire day during a school vacation or when they are ill. This estimate does not even take into account older children in higher grades, nor does it consider that nearly all children are left alone occasionally while parents run brief errands. This statistic may be even higher. It is difficult to get an accurate count of youngsters left alone because, for safety reasons, parents often instruct their children not to tell anyone they are home alone; some parents also deny leaving children alone because of their own guilt feelings.

Even more shocking is the estimate that of all the youngsters home alone, one-third will sometime have to face an emergency situation without the help and protection of an adult. The emergency may be a severe injury, a fire, a stranger following the child home, an assault, a burglary, or even a natural disaster.

When I switched from wilderness training to teaching children how to take care of themselves, I had to develop my own curriculum based on knowledge gained in mothering my two daughters and the many other youngsters who shared our home after school during my ten years as a day-care mother. I also interviewed experts in the fields of pediatrics, child psychology, nutrition, education, and emergency medicine, as well as police and fire professionals. Many parents provided additional information on problems and solutions they had encountered. Finally, I interviewed hundreds of youngsters, mostly between 6 and 16, who generously shared their experiences, concerns, and fears.

Armed with all this information, I have written this book as a guide to help you teach your children how to stay safe and sound. It is only through you that I can reach your vulnerable children. And please believe me, *they are vulnerable.* I am constantly amazed at how many students in my classes are ignorant of even the most basic rules of safety and self-reliance; but it is wonderful to see how eager they are to learn. Youngsters tell me that learning these skills gives them a good feeling of confidence and self-worth.

Throughout this book, you will read the words "your children" and "our children." I do not mean that we parents actually own our youngsters. Essentially they are in our care for just a little while, a few years that pass all too quickly. During this short time, we parents have the important responsibility of teaching our youngsters skills they will use the rest of their lives. One of the most important skills they will ever learn from us is how to keep themselves safe and sound.

Chapter 1

TEACHING YOUR CHILDREN
HOW TO STAY
SAFE AND SOUND

We all know that parents are under a great deal of stress from working, parenting, participating in school and community activities, and just trying to find time to enjoy life. Single parents, especially, are stretched almost to the breaking point each and every day. Yet unquestionably, it is still vital that parents find the time to teach their children the important lessons they need to stay safe and sound. There is no substitute; there is no teacher as effective as a concerned and committed parent.

The Need for Teaching

We adults can easily say that the world today is just not the same world we grew up in. Crime is a larger threat no matter where we live, and no family can consider itself immune to violence or danger. Many more parents are working outside the home, and that means many more children are staying home alone, taking responsibility for themselves. Because of the increased rate of divorce, many youngsters are forced to share parents and homes with children from a previous marriage. Sherri's story will show how important it is for parents to be teachers and establish open lines of communication between themselves and their children.

When Sherri's mother remarried, her new husband and his

two teenage boys moved into the home Sherri had previously shared with her mother. Sherri was unhappy about this turn of events and jealous of the attention her mother paid to the boys. Although she made an outward show of adjustment when the parents were present, during the times before and after school, when the children were alone, Sherri did all she could to make the boys feel like intruders.

One day the boys decided to get even with Sherri. They cornered her in her room and forced her to take off her clothes. They threatened to kill her new kitten if she told anyone. The boys' harassment gradually became worse, but when Sherri tried to tell her mother, she was scolded for making up stories. She soon kept the secret to herself, but felt an increasing guilt because she thought that her silence indicated consent.

One afternoon a neighbor found Sherri crying, and after gentle questioning Sherri revealed what had been happening. When Sherri's mother and stepfather were told, they at first expressed disbelief, but eventually believed Sherri when the boys confessed. Even though the whole family received counseling, Sherri's feelings of guilt and shame can never be erased.

If Sherri's mother had taught her daughter about sexual assault, the child would have been better prepared to deal with the advances of her stepbrothers. Sherri's mother also should have been aware that children very rarely make up stories about sexual assault.

Children do not automatically know about first aid, and unless they are taught, they may not make the correct decisions during a severe emergency. Consider Bob's story.

Bob's family had just moved into a new subdivision where many of the adjoining homes had not yet been sold. Recently, there had been incidents of children breaking into these houses by "bouncing" open the windows—repeatedly hitting them just enough to knock open the locks.

One day when Bob got home from school and realized he did not have his key, he decided to try bouncing open the window. The first try had no effect, but on the second try he broke the glass with his fist and cut himself severely. After climbing through the window, Bob did what the majority of untrained youngsters do in a severe emergency; he called his parents. He couldn't reach his mother at work, so he called his father, told him what had happened, then passed out from loss of blood. Bob's father called the ambulance, then hurried home. Fortunately Bob recovered, but he still has a long scar on his arm.

Bob's injury could have been avoided if the family had previously set up a plan of action in case Bob was locked out. If Bob had been trained in basic first aid, he would have known the importance of phoning immediately for emergency help, instead of wasting time calling his parents and asking them what to do.

Once in a while, parents will ask if it's really necessary to teach their youngsters about personal safety and dealing with strangers; they feel that the children will be unnecessarily frightened. The answer is evident from this story.

Mary's parents didn't want their daughter to hear about strangers and the "scary" things that could happen to an 8-year-old girl. Besides, they lived in a nice suburban area that didn't have much crime, and Mary's mother was at home all day. The last time Mary was seen, she was only a few blocks from home. Two other schoolgirls said that a man in a car had been stopping kids that day to ask directions. Although Mary was reported missing within an hour and an intensive search was conducted by local police and federal authorities, there has been no trace of Mary in over two years. Her parents still do not know what happened to their little girl, who had not been taught to be wary of strangers.

Sometimes parents, unaware of potential safety problems, believe their instructions are adequate. Consider the story of Joan.

When Joan began staying alone after school, her parents told her to find out who was at the door before opening it and warned her not to lose the house key they gave her to wear on a string around her neck.

A man who stopped to watch the schoolchildren saw Joan's key—a sure sign she was going to be alone—and followed her home. Joan unlocked the door, went in, and locked it carefully behind her. He rang the doorbell, and when Joan asked who was there, he said he was delivering an important package. The man sounded friendly, so Joan opened the door. After beating and raping Joan, he burglarized the house.

Joan's parents did not realize the dangers of a child home alone answering the door, nor did they realize how important it was for her to keep the house key out of sight under her shirt.

When parents take the time to teach their youngsters, often the entire family benefits from aired feelings and concerns. My 26-year-old friend, Susan, told me that when she was a child she was so terrified during the time she was left home alone that she locked herself in the bathroom, for hours at a time, and didn't come out until she heard her mother's car pull into the driveway. She felt she couldn't tell her parents about her terrible fear because they praised her so often for being grown up that she didn't want to lose their respect.

If Susan's parents had talked to her about fears, they could have reassured her that these feelings are common and normal when children are home alone. She could have aired her concerns, and the family could have worked on strategies to help Susan conquer her anxiety.

Parents who take the time to prepare their youngsters to stay home alone usually make a greater effort to structure the situation, determining the best arrangement for sibling relations. Consider the story of Sam and his brother Bill.

Even though both brothers are now grown men with families of their own, Sam still thinks his brother Bill is bossy and controlling. This resentment dates back twenty years to the time when the boys were alone every day after school while their father, a widower, worked. Since Bill was the oldest, he assumed charge of his brother, assigned Sam's chores, decided if Sam could play at a friend's house, and even determined if Sam deserved a snack.

If Sam's father had prepared his boys to stay home alone, he might have given greater thought to structuring their relationship, determining who should be in charge. He might have kept closer track of how things were going while he was away at work.

How to Teach

This book is not meant to be tucked away on a shelf and seldom used. It is written as a guide for you to teach your children the skills they need when they're in charge of themselves. Even after these skills have been taught and mastered, the book will serve as a reference source.

The chapters in this book contain many of the role-playing

exercises and activities I have used successfully in my classes. I also encourage you to make up your own to fit your particular situation. Role playing is an effective way to teach youngsters. As an ancient Chinese proverb on learning says: "What I hear, I forget. What I see, I remember. What I do, I understand." Children hear what is going on, act out how they should respond, and practice the correct procedure. Your children will learn and retain the lessons most effectively when you use this multisensory approach. Don't be afraid to "ham it up" when you act out the parts, and don't worry about looking foolish. Your children will be happily surprised to discover that you haven't really forgotten how to pretend.

Set aside a specific time each week, preferably during the early evening hours, when you can sit down with your youngsters and teach them the skills contained in this book. If you make this teaching time an important family commitment, you will be rewarded by seeing your relationship with your children improved. The fun of shared play, and the increased communication and trust that will develop between you and your youngsters will more than make up for the time you have spent. And you will have the peace of mind that comes from knowing you've done everything possible to teach your children how to keep themselves safe and sound.

Chapter 2

DECIDING TO LET YOUR CHILD STAY HOME ALONE

How do you decide when your youngsters are ready to stay home alone? There is no test that will accurately determine a child's readiness to stay home alone. As a parent, you must carefully weigh all factors when considering your offspring's maturity. Each child is unique and should be evaluated as such.

Evaluating Your Child's Readiness

The following questions will help you determine your child's readiness.

1. Is your child enthusiastic and willing to stay home alone or is he hesitant and dreading it? Both enthusiasm and willingness have a large bearing on how successfully a child will manage his time home alone.

2. How old is your child? Most parents believe children in grade 4 and above (10 years or older) can successfully stay alone, but you must assess your own child's maturity, and abilities.

3. Do you have the whole-hearted support of your spouse in this decision? Ideally, both parents should make this decision together. If one parent disagrees, the venture is less likely to succeed.

4. Are there any medical conditions such as epilepsy or asthma that could make staying home alone dangerous for your child? If such a condition exists, would you be able to work out an emergency plan for your child to get help? Would it be possible for your child to deal with the condition by herself?

5. Is this a particularly stressful period for you or your child? If so, realize that you might be adding even more stress by letting the child stay home alone. It might be better to let your life get back to normal before your child begins self-care.

6. Are you or your spouse easily reached by phone during the time your child will be alone? In general, supervisors are aware of a working parent's need to communicate with children at home alone, and are willing to cooperate if they are asked. If it is difficult for you to take calls at work, perhaps a coworker could occasionally handle your child's calls. In that situation, it is helpful if your child and the coworker meet, so they will be more than just voices on the phone. Be sure to furnish your coworker with a list of your children's names and ages, home address, emergency phone numbers for your area, neighbors' phones, doctor's phone, and any other information that might be needed.

7. Is your home safe? Most families find they need to spend money on additional safety equipment such as smoke alarms, fire extinguishers, and good locks for doors and windows.

8. Is your neighborhood safe? Take a tour of your own neighborhood and see if there are safety problems such as empty buildings, secluded wooded areas, abandoned refrigerators, or other potential dangers. Walk the route your child takes to school and check your own yard for safety hazards.

9. Are there trusted neighbors who are home during the time your child will be alone? Would they be willing to be called upon in case of need? It certainly helps if your child already has a good relationship with the neighbors. Realize that you may have to pay a neighbor to watch out for your child or to be an emergency contact for the youngster. If you have just moved into a new apartment or neighborhood, make sure you and your child meet at least a few of your neighbors.

10. How long will your child be alone? Remember to include your commuting time when you figure up the time you will be away from home. Generally children are able to stay home alone up to three hours without mishap or excessive loneliness.

11. Will your child need to prepare meals? You should determine how you feel about having your child use the stove and other kitchen appliances when you are not there to supervise. Most children can easily make their own snacks and lunches, but it's better if they have some help with breakfast and dinner; otherwise, those meals may be inadequate or even nonexistent.

12. Will your youngster be able to continue after-school activities such as sports, clubs, and music or dancing lessons? Since children home alone often feel isolated, after-school functions are important because they enhance a child's specific skills and help develop his social involvement.

13. What care arrangements can you make if your child is ill and must stay home from school? You may also have to work out contingency plans for school holidays and vacations months in advance.

14. Does your child convey her feelings and concerns to you, or does she keep them hidden? Since you will be away more, you will have less time for communication, yet this interaction will become even more vital to both of you. It takes special effort to foster communication.

15. Does your child have an abnormal amount of fear? Children home alone are naturally more fearful than those supervised by an adult, but the way a child deals with such fear, positively or negatively, has a long-term effect on personality development.

16. Is your child an only child, or will he be home with one or more siblings? The advantage in having one child caring for himself is that sibling arguments and fights will be avoided. On the other hand, two or more children home alone experience less loneliness and boredom. Statistics show there is also safety in numbers.

17. Is your child in a family that has merged through remarriage? Stepchildren do not share a common bond or history and must deal with territorialism, competition, and power struggles. Also, the risk of sexual assault or exploitation is much greater when stepchildren are left alone together. All these factors aggravate the normal day-to-day disagreements and make it more important that such situations be closely monitored.

18. If you have more than one child, will one be in charge, or will both be independent agents answerable only to parents and not to each other? Your decision should be based on the difference in ages between the youngsters and their individual personalities. It is important to address this question right from the start, so your kids will know clearly what is expected of them.

19. Do your children usually get along with each other when you are home? Generally, if children get along reasonably well when you are home, they will get along together when you are not home. Unfortunately the opposite is also true.

20. Does your youngster purposely defy your authority very often? Does he exhibit behavior that is considered abnormal? Has he ever been involved in drugs, alcohol, shoplifting, setting fires, or any other behavior of extreme concern? Psychologists say children who have already exhibited these tendencies are almost certain to get into trouble when home alone. Such children are better off with adult supervision or in a structured day-care center. If this is impossible and you must leave a child like this alone, he should be monitored more often. If you cannot physically check on his behavior, make sure you can phone him frequently.

21. Can you trust your child to have complete and unchaperoned access to all areas of your home while you are away? When kids are alone, they may be tempted to explore areas of the home that are off limits and delve into things you thought were safely hidden. Even locked cupboards and closets aren't always safe.

22. Last, but most important, will your child be trained to handle the emergencies as well as the everyday problems that arise when she is alone? Children who have been taught the skills outlined in this book are far safer, more confident, and successful when home alone.

Benefits and Drawbacks of Self-Care

Before children begin to stay home alone, it is wise for parents to be aware of both the positive and negative aspects of self-care. With this knowledge you can develop the positive qualities and at the same time work to avoid pitfalls.

A growing sense of independence, maturity, and competence are the greatest benefits when children take care of themselves. Staying home alone is one of the first steps on the road to independence and eventual separation of children from parents. Children can enjoy this excursion into the world of adults, yet be secure in the knowledge that their responsibilities are limited and they will still be taken care of by their parents.

Being home alone can prepare children practically and emotionally for a time in the future when they will be on their own. They will have a heightened sense of self-esteem from knowing that they can competently care for themselves in most situations. They will also be aware of the positive contribution they are making to the family in terms of finances and time by doing some cooking, cleaning, or even laundry. Other benefits may include better report cards because of added time to do homework or a developing proficiency in a sport or hobby.

On the negative side, unsupervised youngsters are exposed to dangerous situations that they must handle on their own: fire, physical injury, robbery, accidents, abduction, and sexual assault. As a result, youngsters home alone also experience a higher-than-normal amount of stress and fear. They often experience an increased sense of loneliness, isolation, and boredom, and their social skills sometimes lag behind those of their peers who have more chance to interact with adults or other children.

Because parents and children are separated so much of the time, communication is usually decreased. It takes time to effectively interact with a child, and working parents are often short of both time and patience. In some cases, unsupervised children who are bored may be tempted to experiment with drugs, alcohol, sex, or other undesirable activities. If self-care turns out to be a bad experience for a child, it may disrupt all his or her remaining childhood years and even continue into adulthood. Damage once done is hard to undo.

How to Begin Self-Care

Gradually and slowly is the recommended way to begin letting children take care of themselves. This makes it less stressful for both child and parents. Begin self-care by first visiting at the apartment next door or across the back fence while your child plays in the house. You will be within calling distance if you are needed. Later, try going farther, but be sure to tell your child where you are so he or she can reach you if the need arises. Later on, extend your trips away from home by going to the grocery store, taking a baby-sitter home, or running an errand. Then leave the youngster alone for longer periods of time—perhaps for an hour after school.

Unfortunately, the way most families enter into self-care is not a deliberate or well-thought-out process. Usually the decision is made abruptly, under stress, because of a change in the family status which produces the need for additional income, such as a death, divorce, or loss of a job. It may also occur when current child-care arrangements are abruptly terminated. Such changes bring about a predictable increase in household stress, and a time of unusual stress is not the ideal time to embark on a new arrangement.

However, if it is simply unavoidable, there are ways to help smooth the sailing. First, to reduce stress, simplify your schedules and routines for at least the first month. Cancel or reschedule evening meetings and appointments, eat more meals out, or make home meals simple. Arrange to spend your evenings with your offspring, teaching them the skills outlined in this book and just being available if they want to share concerns or feelings. Being an understanding and sympathetic parent can certainly ease an abrupt transition into self-care.

On occasion, youngsters beset by peer pressure will ask to stay home alone. Schoolmates may be ridiculing them for having a baby-sitter after school, or for having to attend an organized day-care program. Even though the child is happy with the present situation, he may not want to appear too young to stay home unsupervised. Once a child has started staying home alone, it may be difficult for him to admit it has turned out to be less desirable than he imagined. He may think he will lose face if he backs out of the new arrangement.

If your child asks to stay home alone, and it is at all possible, make it clear to him that you will try self-care on a trial basis only and that you will pursue other child-care options if self-care does not work out satisfactorily. If children are assured that the arrangement is not permanent, they will be more honest in discussing their reaction to staying home alone.

Assessing the Trial Run

After a two-week trial period, it is advisable for you and your child to assess the self-care experience. Be cautious about excessively praising a youngster for staying home alone; many children will not own up to having problems for fear they will lose their parents' respect and praise. They also might not complain because they fear adding to the burdens their parents already bear. Sometimes children cannot envision any positive solution to their problems and may consider them to be hopeless. As a parent, you have to be persistent to learn your child's true feelings about self-care. You have to convince kids there are solutions for every problem, no matter how insurmountable the difficulties seem. Gently probe for your child's responses until you are sure you really know your child's true feelings about staying home alone.

If you find that self-care is not a good family situation, consider exploring these other options.

1. Look into programs such as boys and girls clubs, local YMCAs, or regular day-care centers that offer before- and after-school supervision.

2. Find a trusted teenager or a neighbor who would like to make some extra money to care for your child.

3. Advertise for a senior citizen who may need or want a job.

4. Ask the mothers of other youngsters in your child's school if they would consider letting your child play at their house for a few hours after school. You may be able to trade services in lieu of money—a barter system.

These options cost more than self-care, but may be well worth the money if self-care is not successful and becomes stressful to your family. Having multiple options helps ensure that you are not locked into making your child stay home alone. Usually when children begin to stay alone on a regular basis, this arrangement becomes permanent. It is easy to get the family into self-care but difficult to get out of it unless both parents and children are jolted by problems so severe they force a change.

In Conclusion

The success of a self-care arrangement depends heavily on the preparations that are made before the children actually begin to stay home alone. Using the twenty-two questions in this chapter as a guide, parents should first decide whether or not their youngsters have the maturity and ability to take care of themselves. Then, with an awareness of both the benefits and drawbacks of self-care, the family must begin to carefully set up rules and arrangements for the situation. The following chapter will help you begin to structure your individual self-care situation.

Chapter 3

GETTING STARTED

Once you have made the decision to leave your children at home alone, your next step should be to carefully set up the rules and determine the arrangements that your children are to follow when they are in charge of themselves. This chapter will provide some helpful guidelines.

Setting House Rules

It is vital to establish a set of rules for the youngsters to follow when they are home alone. The most effective way to set up these rules is to schedule a family meeting where you can discuss the rules, be sure they are clear and easily understood by everyone involved, then prepare a copy for each person. Ask each of your children to sign the sheet to indicate that they understand all the rules and will try to abide by them. This makes house rules an important contract between parents and children and lessens the chances of the children complaining that they really didn't understand what was expected when they broke a rule.

Your rules should be posted in a prominent place, such as on the refrigerator or family bulletin board. Make sure that your youngsters acquaint their friends with these rules and let them know they are also expected to follow the rules when they are in your home.

The following rules are those most commonly adopted by families involved in self-care.

1. Come directly home after school. Phone a parent or your contact person when you come in so adults know you are home safely.

2. Keep the door locked at all times. Do not answer the door if someone rings the bell or knocks (unless you have been instructed differently).

3. Change into play clothes when you come home.

4. Only have friends in the house with parental permission.

5. Call parents before you go anywhere to ask permission and let them know where you will be.

6. You may (or may not) play outdoors in the following areas: (*specifically designate which areas are okay*).

7. Limit phone calls to less than ten minutes every hour so parents can call home if they need to.

8. Try to find other activities to keep you busy besides watching TV. After you've done your homework, you may watch TV for _____ hours.

9. Do your assigned chores.

10. Use only those appliances you have permission to use when you are alone.

11. Try to get along with siblings. If you cannot come to an agreement on something, drop the matter until parents are home.

12. In a real emergency, call _____ first, then call parents.

Many parents add a personal note to their rules such as "Please do not do anything that endangers your safety, health, or security. You know what is right and what is wrong. Make good choices and live up to our trust and faith in you."

Mornings Home Alone

When youngsters are home alone in the mornings, there are some special matters and arrangements that parents need to be aware of. The first concern is getting youngsters up in the morning. If parents must leave for work before their children are up, they should either leave an alarm set or be able to call home after they arrive at work. Let's face it, a personal call is a much nicer way for a child to wake up and is probably more reliable than an alarm, which can easily be shut off.

The second concern is breakfast. On their own, children often eat a woefully inadequate breakfast. Parents can help by setting out the foods ahead of time or by giving youngsters money to buy breakfast at school, if the school serves this meal. Breakfasts at home do not have to be hot cereal or the traditional bacon and eggs, especially if time is limited and you do not want your children using the stove. For instance, a bowl of nutritious cold cereal or a peanut butter and jelly sandwich, a glass of milk, and an apple or orange are very adequate.

Clothing and grooming are the third concern when children are alone before school. Teachers tell me they often know who is home alone in the mornings just by the way the students are dressed. Many of the unsupervised youngsters either are not adequately clothed for the day's weather, or wear the same outfit day after day, or wear clothing that is clearly inappropriate. Quite often the child's personal grooming is sadly neglected. Parents can help by laying out their children's schoolwear the previous night or before leaving for work in the morning. If it looks like rain, put out a raincoat and umbrella. You can also teach your kids to make a regular habit of brushing their teeth, washing their face and hands, and combing their hair in the morning.

Assuming the responsibility for getting together whatever supplies and equipment are needed for the day is the fourth concern. Library books, gym clothes, homework assignments, field trip permission slips, and special projects all must be remembered and taken to school by the youngsters. Parents can help by setting out the needed equipment ahead of time and reminding the child with a quick phone call home before he or she leaves for school.

Since getting up, eating breakfast, dressing, and collecting supplies usually must be completed in a short length of time, children are under a great deal of stress in the mornings. Thoughtful parents can certainly help alleviate the pressure, but there will probably be times when children on their own will be late for school. Many schools require a note from an adult explaining the tardiness. Since children in self-care are not likely to be able to produce such a note, their stress may be increased to the point where they would rather stay home than deal with the problem. A child may even call a parent and report that he is ill. Parents at work can hardly assess a child's physical condition and usually permit the child to stay home. Once a pattern like this becomes established, it is hard to break. Parents should always be sure the school's secretary, principal, and teacher are aware that the youngster is home alone in the mornings. Once the school officials understand the situation, they are almost always more lenient and willing to cooperate by postponing a written note or phoning a parent at work. It is also a good idea to ask school authorities to let you know if there are recurrent problems with tardiness, so you can deal with the problem before it becomes too well established. If your youngsters ride a bus to school, try to line up a neighbor they can call for a ride if they miss the bus, but make sure your children do not abuse this arrangement.

Sibling Concerns

There are both blessings and drawbacks to families with more than one child. Siblings home together generally aren't as lonely as an only child might be, but the potential for fights and arguments is there.

Deciding Who Is in Charge

For sibling self-care to be successful, your children must know who is in charge when they are home alone together. To make this decision, consider the following points.

1. When siblings are close to the same age, ideally neither one should be put in charge. There will be less bossing and fighting if your children are independent agents in charge of their own actions and accountable only to parents.

2. When siblings are separated in age by three years or more, it is often successful to put the older in charge of the younger. If you make this a formal baby-sitting arrangement with a set wage, you can expect more and have more say about it because you are paying for the service.

You must watch to be sure the older child doesn't act like a surrogate parent or become too bossy or domineering. Your home rules should already be set up so the younger child understands that it is the parents who have made the rules, not the sibling baby-sitter. Also make it a policy that you, not the older sibling, will deal with any disobedience of the younger child. Advance parental planning of chores, snacks, and activities also limits the domineering and decision making to be done by the older child.

There is a tendency, especially among single parents, to treat the older child as an equal partner in the upbringing and care of the younger sibling. This relationship is not appropriate, nor is it fair to the older child, who should be able to enjoy his childhood years, which go by too fast as it is. Try to make other arrangements for the younger child's care at least once a week so the older child has time off to pursue his own interests and to socialize with friends of his own age.

Be certain that the younger child is properly trained so she can handle any problems if she is alone. Many parents train only the older child, when actually both children need to know how to deal with everyday dilemmas and true dangers.

Helping Siblings Get Along Together

If your youngsters have been taught to get along together and try to resolve their conflicts with compromise and negotiation, they will generally do the same when unsupervised. Parents can help siblings get along even better by emphasizing how fortunate they are to have a loving relationship with a brother or sister. When children are complimented for getting along well, it provides them with positive reinforcement, and they actually begin to believe it and act accordingly. Although it does not happen overnight, this reinforcement can often work wonders. Be careful not to lay the compliments on too thickly, or your children will realize you are deliberately using this strategy. At times when your kids are getting along well, try out some of the comments below:

"You and your sister are such good friends. I wish my brother and I had been able to cooperate and get along like you guys do. We never even got to know one another very well because we were always fighting."

"You two have a super way of working things out. Did you know that's not real common among brothers?"

"You children get along much better than most kids your age. You even seem to be each other's best friends."

"You know, you kids don't seem to fight as much as you used to. You're really acting a lot more grown up."

"Other mothers tell me how lucky I am to have girls like you who get along together so well. I really am lucky to have such super kids."

Sibling Rivalry and Fights

No matter how well adjusted and loving siblings are, and no matter how carefully parents arrange to alleviate potential conflicts, there will be some disagreements and fights when children are unsupervised. Fighting is only a real cause for worry if children physically injure each other, or if one child becomes a bully and constantly gets his own way.

When sibling fights do occur, parents should try to stay out of them and let the kids know that their fights are their own problem. You can help them see that it is to their advantage to get along, since fighting simply wastes time that could be better spent doing more enjoyable things. When they do fight, encourage your children to follow these rules; it will help if you and your spouse do the same when you are in disagreement.

1. Make an effort to work out small problems before they escalate into major battles. Encourage children to express their feelings and speak up when something is beginning to bother them. If they let off steam gradually, they aren't as likely to blow up.

2. Do not call parents at work for small disputes; phone them only if the problem is very serious and needs immediate attention. If the children are not able to come to an agreement or compromise on a small problem, they should put it on hold until parents are home to advise or referee.

3. Remember the timeless adage, "More flies can be attracted with honey than with vinegar." Explain to your children that this means they will be more apt to get what they want if they are nice about it and resist the temptation to yell or fight.

4. If a situation becomes unbearable, remove yourself. Before you explode, it is wise to go into another room until you calm down. Try deep breathing, counting to 10, or even punching a pillow.

5. Avoid name calling or bringing up past problems or fights. When you remain civil and stay centered on the present problem only, it is easier to reach a solution.

6. Remember there are always two sides to every story. When you have stated your views, you must be willing to listen to the other person's side, too. Usually both parties think they are in the right, when actually both are partly right and partly wrong.

7. No one has to "win" an argument. To reach an agreement, usually both parties have to give in, so there is no actual winner or loser.

8. After the argument is over and both sides have cooled down, discuss what has been learned from the experience. Think what you would change about the clash if you could replay it. Think how you could behave better the next time a similar argument occurs.

9. Remember, when you fight with a family member, you cannot walk away from it and go home. Family members have to live together day in and day out, and it is no fun for everyone to remain tense for a long time after a major battle. Real families are not like those on TV who can fight, settle the argument, and end up loving each other, all during a brief half hour, so weigh the cost before you fight with a family member.

Fostering Good Communication

Working parents have less time for communication and interaction with their children, yet this vital part of parenting is even more important when most of the day is spent apart. Working parents have to make a special effort to keep the lines of communication open.

Your children may discourage your efforts to initiate conversation with such noncommittal answers as: "Everything's OK," "Oh, nothing," "Yeah, just fine." One effective way to combat this is to ask leading questions that cannot be answered with just a few words. Try some of these:

"What's the best thing that happened to you today?"

"What was the scariest thing that happened to you today?"

"What event made you feel proud of yourself either at home or at school?"

"What would you like to change about staying home alone?"

"What would you most like to change about (*choose one*) me, your father, yourself, a teacher, your sibling, etc.?"

"What worried you the most today?"

"Who did you play with at recess and what did you do?"

"Who did you eat lunch with?"

"Who did you ride with on the school bus and what did you talk about?"

Questions like those are more apt to get an answer, but if you still get the "I don't know" responses, be patient. Assure your children that you really are interested, then repeat the question, making sure you are giving your undivided attention.

One very special father in my neighborhood, who went to work before his children awoke, made it a practice to leave illustrated love notes for his sons to read while they ate breakfast. After his death at a young age, the father's cherished notes were compiled into a heartwarming book called *Love, Dad.**

Another method I have found for giving complete attention to a child is to take the youngster for a walk. I take each of my daughters, separately, on a short walk; sometimes it is just around the block. I get needed exercise and each girl gets time with me away from the rest of the family. During these walks we talk over all sorts of things, from growing up to the merits of blueberry bubble gum. The girls know they have my complete attention and we both cherish these special times.

The Single Child Home Alone

If you have only one child home alone, you too can count your blessings! You will not have to deal with sibling fights and arguments. But there are also drawbacks. Complaints about loneliness, boredom, and isolation are the ones most often mentioned by the single child home alone and by parents who are concerned with making self-care a successful and positive program.

Although these three factors are important, they can be minimized by providing the single child with planned activities that occupy at least one afternoon a week. Camp Fire Girls, Boy Scouts, church clubs, and sports groups are some of the common options. Ask your local school, YMCA, pastor, or city recreation department about other programs for children. After-school classes in music, drama, dance, or other subjects are often available.

Some of these activities require transportation; this can present problems when parents work. It is often possible to arrange for a ride with parents of your children's friends. You might suggest having a car pool or arrange to pay for the gas if it is not possible to share driving responsibilities. Public transportation is a good option for older children.

---

* Patrick Connolly, *Love, Dad,* Universal Press, Kansas City, Missouri, 1985.

Try to make arrangements for your child to spend an afternoon and evening at a friend's house once a week or at least on an occasional basis. If your child complains she doesn't have any friends, ask her teacher or room mother for suggestions. Either arrange to pay for this time or be sure to reciprocate by having the friend spend a night at your house or go on a special outing with you and your child.

Try to find someone in your neighborhood your child can visit if she feels unbearably lonesome. Many older women are home all day and would welcome company, but be sure your child does not become a nuisance.

Coming home to an empty house can be a bleak and lonely experience for a single child, but parents can do some things to make a child's homecoming a positive experience. A love note left for the youngster to find after school makes a nice welcome home. When your child phones to say he's safely home, try to spend a few minutes visiting with him and let him tell you about his day at school. Perhaps you can arrange to come directly home from work to pick up your child and take him with you when you do your grocery shopping or run necessary errands.

In Conclusion

The majority of self-care arrangements, whether for one child or more, are positive childhood experiences. Fortunately, most parents realize they cannot simply walk out the door, leaving their youngsters alone, so they are willing to invest the time and thought it takes to make self-care a positive experience for the whole family.

Chapter 4

SAFE AND SOUND AT HOME ALONE

Fortunately, most of the time children spend by themselves passes in a safe, mundane routine, but there are times when being alone can be a terrifying and dangerous experience, even for the most mature and well-adjusted youngsters. Parents can help by teaching their children how to handle potentially dangerous situations and by discussing fear and teaching youngsters how to handle this powerful emotion.

It is important for parents to understand that children left home unsupervised will suffer more fear than children who have an adult handy to explain away the frightening noises and cope with dangerous situations. Fear is a common emotion in all humans, no matter what age. Fear is useful when it keeps us out of trouble, but bothersome when it gets in our way and prevents us from doing things we want to do.

How to Help Your Child Handle Fear

Think back to the time you were your child's age. Did you hate the dark? Were you ever afraid of monsters, bogeymen, or bears under your bed? Did the noise of the furnace heating up sound like someone creeping down the hall? Admit to your children that you had such fears when you were young. It helps kids to know that their fears are not abnormal and that they can talk about them with their parents. This dialogue then opens the door to exploring ways children can cope with fears.

1. If what your child fears is a real possibility, take steps to prevent it from becoming a reality. For example, if your child is afraid of losing the house key, help him find ways to take good care of it or relieve his fears by leaving a spare key with a neighbor or in a safe hiding place at home.

2. If what your youngster fears is not a real possibility, such as sharks in the bathtub, just talking about this fear in an understanding way will usually show how unreal it is. Be sure not to laugh at your child's fears, because even a shark in the tub may seem very real to a child.

3. Often just knowing how to handle a scary situation defuses fear. If your children know where a working flashlight is, their fear of a blackout is lessened. If they worry about being injured, knowledge of first aid will give them greater confidence.

4. Make sure that your youngsters don't fuel their imaginations by watching spooky television shows or reading horror stories.

5. Having a friend over or even visiting on the phone is helpful when children are afraid. It's amazing how fears can vanish when two children are busy playing or chatting.

6. Keeping busy also helps fearful youngsters cope with being alone. Kids who are involved with hobbies, projects, homework, or even chores will experience less fear.

7. Pets in the house are a great source of comfort and security to children. Many police departments recommend a dog for a security safeguard, but even a kitten or gerbil provides some comfort.

8. Conducting a regular security check of doors and windows to make sure they are locked will make youngsters feel safer and more secure at home alone.

9. If house noises scare your child, a radio tuned to a quiet music station will help cover these sounds. I hesitate to suggest turning on the TV, because it easily becomes an all-consuming activity.

10. Many children find praying relieves their fear. They find comfort in talking to a supreme being they regard as a shelter and protection for big and small alike.

Sometime during their childhood, most children will hide from things they fear. If your child hides regularly, talk with her about it in a matter-of-fact, noncondemning way. Kids feel badly enough about this sort of behavior without parents belittling them and eroding their self-confidence even further. Work on the listed suggestions for coping with fears and let your child know you support her efforts to overcome fear. A few lapses may occur now and then, but with parental support, encouragement, and positive solutions, most children soon give up hiding altogether.

Two Main Fears for Children Home Alone

No matter where they live, two fears are common to all children who spend time alone. The first is dealing with someone at the door, and the second is handling phone calls, especially frightening ones. Because we teach our children to be polite to adults, these situations are particularly stressful, since children aren't sure how to balance good manners and personal safety concerns. For this reason, it is vital that parents set firm rules for answering doors and handling phone calls. I have found that children are least prepared to deal with these two situations, yet the skills required in dealing with them are among the easiest to master.

Someone at the Door

During my classes, I ask youngsters to imagine that they are home alone; then I knock on their pretend door to see how they will handle the situation. Some youngsters simply open the imaginary door without a trace of caution or concern. Some children ask, "Who is it?" while others pretend to look out a window or peephole to see who is there. Some keep the chain on while opening the door. These children are either following their parents' instructions or trying to do what they think is safe, yet all of these actions actually put them in danger!

Most of us know that opening a door wide to strangers is just asking for trouble, but lots of parents do not realize that opening a door partway is almost as dangerous. A person of even moderate strength can push a door hard enough to rip a chain off the wooden frame. A child peeking out a window can often be seen by the person at the door, who may correctly suspect the child is home alone. When a caller hears a childish voice ask, "Who is it?" it is a safe guess that the youngster is home alone. Most peepholes are not at a child's height and a caller hearing a chair dragged to the door will know it's a child climbing up to look through the peephole.

Most police departments and safety professionals recommend that *children alone should ignore a doorbell or a knock.* Any other action puts the youngsters in danger or forces them to decide whether or not the person at the door is safe to admit. It's unfair to expect children to make this decision by themselves. After years of teaching safety skills to youngsters, I know how easy it is to talk them into opening the door. Kids want to be helpful and polite, and those intending to harm a child know this and use it to their advantage. Criminals can easily feign an emergency or say they are making a delivery, and most of the time they can talk a child into opening the door.

Some parents give their offspring a list of people who can be admitted, but this creates difficulty, because before the children can open the door, they have to ask who is there. If the caller is not on the "safe list," the children are stuck with handling this uncomfortable situation. That's putting too much responsibility on youngsters who want to be polite but also know they should be cautious.

When I tell children in my classes to ignore doorbells and knocks when they are alone, there is always a hand raised to ask what to do when parents are locked out or a best friend comes over to play. My answer is that parents who are locked out will usually shout to make themselves known. Since best friends usually know their buddies are not allowed to answer the door when they're alone, they can phone in advance or stand outside and holler to get their friend's attention. Some youngsters devise a secret-code knock for family and friends. That's fine as long as the code is actually kept secret, but youngsters should be sure it cannot be heard by someone lurking near the door.

REPAIRPEOPLE OR DELIVERIES

Parents expecting a repairperson should try to schedule the call for a time when they will be home. If that's not possible, ask a neighbor to be there. If a delivery is expected, it's far safer if an adult can be home to accept it. You might ask the agency to simply leave the package on the doorstep or in your apartment lobby without your signature, or have it sent to your neighbor's address. Don't make your kids deal with this kind of a situation.

POTENTIAL TROUBLE

There's always the chance a younger child who doesn't know the rule about answering the door may open the door wide before the child in charge gets there. If the situation looks threatening, the child in charge should make the caller think there's an adult in the house or apartment. Here are some examples of how this can be done.

Holler, "Dad, Uncle Bob, there's someone at the door." Tell the person at the door to wait while you get your dad or Uncle Bob, then shut and lock the door on the stranger.

Say, "Let me close the door to keep the dog in, and I'll get my dad." Then quickly close and lock the door.

Simply slam and lock the door on the unwanted caller. If the person does not leave immediately, call the police.

DISPLAYING THE FAMILY NAME

Outdoor signs that list the names of family members can be a safety threat. Recently, in my neighborhood, a potential burglar told such a convincing story about being an old family friend, using first names of family members, the boy who was home alone almost unlocked the door to let him in. Fortunately the child's mother phoned home just then and recognized that the so-called family friend at the door was an imposter, so she called the police. If that boy had been taught to ignore the doorbell when he was at home alone or if the family had removed the outdoor sign with first names, this potentially dangerous situation would not have arisen.

Last names on mailboxes or doormats do not give as much detailed information to outsiders, but many families have wisely removed even these.

Dealing with Phone Calls

It is important that parents give their offspring definite guidelines for handling various kinds of phone calls. This helps lessen children's fear and increase their confidence when they are home alone.

The best way for anyone, and especially children, to answer the home phone is to simply say, "Hello." It is no longer a good idea to teach children to say, "This is the Jones residence, Jenny speaking." That may sound polite, but we do not want our children to identify our family or to be on a first-name basis with a stranger, even a stranger on the phone. When the phone rings and the caller asks to speak to Mom or Dad, the child who has not been trained otherwise is apt to say Mom and Dad are at work and won't be home until such and such a time. Unfortunately, this lets the caller know the child is home alone and if the caller has access to a phone book, he can obtain your name and address, too. The caller can also assume the child who is careless about giving out information on the phone is also careless about locking doors or letting strangers into the home. Therefore, children not properly trained can easily put themselves in danger.

When asked if Mom or Dad is home, some children say he or she is "busy" or "unavailable." Often this reply just does not sound convincing. Help your youngsters to make up an excuse that sounds like you are in the house or close by, but unable to come to the phone. Here are some believable ones: "Mom (or Dad) is...

In the shower

Taking a bath

Changing the baby

Talking on another phone line

Out in the yard talking to a neighbor

Taking a nap and asked not to be awakened

Mowing the lawn

Painting the living room ceiling

Cleaning the attic or basement

After practicing some of these excuses with your child, you may want a coworker or trusted friend to phone home when you're not there to see how convincing your child sounds. These excuses sound simple, but without practice, your child may get mixed up or sound unconvincing.

Occasionally youngsters decide to make these excuses more realistic by running water in the shower or imitating Dad's deep voice. Those ruses are too complicated and usually ineffective. It's not necessary for kids to stage an elaborate dramatic production just to convince a caller that parents are nearby.

It bothers some children to say that Mom or Dad is in the shower, etc., when their parents really are not even home. Although this "white lie" is for the child's protection, there are some children and parents who refuse to use fibs. If this is the case at your house, there is an alternative, although it is more difficult, takes a lot of careful parental coaching, and can be confusing for most children under age 9.

Here's what to do: When the phone rings, and the caller asks for the parents, instruct your child to put the phone down, take a few steps and holler, "Mom (or Dad), telephone," just as loudly as she would do if you were actually home. Next she should slowly count to 10, then go back and pick up the phone and tell the caller, "Mom (or Dad) just can't come to the phone right now, can I take a message and have her (him) call you back?" The situation could become difficult if the caller asks the child to relay a message to the parent he believes is nearby. In this case, the child could repeat the procedure and again tell the caller she will just have to take a message and have the parent return the call.

As a very last resort, if children are totally flustered and don't know what to say, they can always simply hang up on the caller. It is not a good idea to tell children never to answer the phone, since an unanswered phone can give burglars an indication no one is home. Parents also need to be able to reach their children by phone.

Wrong-number calls are usually just that—a wrong number. When a child answers a wrong-number call, the caller will often ask, "What number did I reach?" Teach your children not to give out your phone number; they should simply tell the caller that he reached a wrong number, then hang up.

If your children get many calls where a person hangs up when the phone is answered, it might be a good idea to let your police department know. A series of such calls could be someone checking to see if the house is occupied. A series of wrong-number calls could also indicate the same thing.

To a child home alone, a nonworking phone can be especially frightening, since the phone can be the youngster's most important lifeline to the outside world. Children should be told what to do if they pick up the phone and the line is dead. Instruct them to check other phones in the house to make sure they are properly hung up and not accidentally off the hook. If that's not the problem, children should hang up for a few minutes and then try again. If the phone still does not operate properly, they may have to go to a neighbor's and call the phone repair number to report the problem. During an interruption of phone service, make sure your child knows to call you at work from a neighbor's or a pay phone so that you won't be worried if you call home and get no answer.

We all know what a prank call is because we probably made them ourselves when we were kids. Although these calls are usually harmless, they can be frightening to children home alone. Since such calls are also common, it's wise to teach youngsters how to handle them. The instructions are simple—hang up! Your children should not laugh or talk to the caller because that only encourages him to phone again. Also caution your children against making prank calls, even in fun, because prank calls are against the law.

An obscene call is when the caller asks sexual or personal questions that are none of his business, talks about sex, or says bad words. From polling my students, I have found that these calls are quite common and are also very frightening to youngsters home alone. Be sure to reassure your children that obscene calls are rarely dangerous. If your youngsters receive an obscene call, tell them not to listen or talk, but to hang up quietly at the first indication that the call is not legitimate. When children hang up quietly without listening, the caller does not achieve his objective of shocking and frightening and will probably give up and call someone else. Most police departments advise against blowing a whistle, hollering, or responding to these calls in any way other than simply hanging up the phone.

If the caller should phone again, the child should again quietly hang up the phone. If there are more calls, the child should unplug the phone or leave it off the hook. I tell my students to phone their parents first to let them know why the phone is off the hook so that they won't become alarmed and think something is wrong at home. If obscene calls persist, contact your local police department and request that a trace be put on your phone. If such a trace is installed, make sure youngsters know what to do if an obscene call comes in while the equipment is on the line.

A threatening call is more serious than a prank or obscene call. If a caller should threaten to harm or even kill, instruct your child to hang up and immediately phone the police. It may also be comforting for the youngster to phone a nearby neighbor who can come over and stay with the child. Threatening calls are usually more frightening than dangerous. When you're talking about how to handle threatening calls, you might mention how much trouble a person (or a child) can get into for making such a call. It's no laughing matter—it's a police matter.

When kids are home alone they also have the job of taking messages for the whole family. When taking a message, teach your children to say something like this: "Mom is taking a shower right now (*or other excuse*). May I take a message and have her call you." The child should be instructed to write down the caller's name, phone number, and message, then read it back to ensure accuracy. Simply memorizing the information usually results in garbled messages, mad parents, and plenty of problems. Make it easier for your children by keeping a pad of paper and several pencils right near the phone. It is also helpful to designate a special place, such as a bulletin board or magnet on the refrigerator, where messages can be posted.

House Keys, Doors, Locks, and Burglars

Problems with house keys and getting locked out worry most youngsters who come home alone. Fortunately there is a great deal parents can do to ease these concerns. First of all, if your children wear their house key on a string or chain around their neck, make sure they keep the "key necklace" hidden under their shirt. Keys dangling around a child's neck can also be dangerous if they get caught in play equipment. Many youngsters thread their pants belt through their key ring, then slip the keys into their pants pocket, out of sight. Others pin the key inside a coat pocket, a backpack, or book bag. Any of these methods helps keep the key secure and out of sight. A plainly visible house key tells any observer that the youngster is going to be home alone, and you don't want your kids to advertise this.

Even youngsters who are careful with their keys occasionally get locked out, so all families should prepare for this situation in advance by deciding on a lock-out plan. Here are some ideas. Leave a spare key with a next-door neighbor who is usually home when your children get home from school. If you live in an apartment, leave a key with the apartment superintendent or a neighbor.

If you decide to hide a key at home, never hide it under the doormat, near or above the door, in or under a flowerpot near the door, or in the mailbox. Those are the first places burglars check and all too often that's exactly where they find the key! If you must hide a house key, put it in a waterproof container and bury it away from the door or hide it under dense shrubbery or even in a neighbor's yard. It is also a good idea to change the hiding place every so often, when it becomes known to many friends or baby-sitters.

If your child gets locked out and there is no spare key available, he should go to a neighbor's or friend's home and phone you at work for instructions. It's not a good idea for the youngster to leave you a note on the door. That's a sure giveaway that the house is unoccupied.

It is the parents' responsibility to make the home as safe as possible for their children, yet many youngsters go home to a house that's not locked. I often hear comments such as: "Dad always leaves the basement door open for me." "Mom leaves the apartment door unlocked." "The door from the garage to the house is always unlocked." "I just push open my window if I forget the key." Parents should realize that intruders can also enter the home through those same unlocked doors and windows. Statistics prove that no neighborhood is immune to break-in, burglary, and even murder. There isn't a street in the United States today that is completely safe from crime, and there is no way to guarantee crime will not occur on your street, or even in your very own home. No matter where you live, lock the doors while you're away. Don't take a chance with the lives of your loved ones.

Don't be like Mrs. Rivera who decided to simply leave the back door unlocked while she was away at work because her kids kept losing their keys. One afternoon when her daughters came home from school, they heard noises in the living room and were horrified to see a strange man grab a filled pillowcase and run out the front door. The girls had surprised a burglar who was ransacking their home! The police officers who responded to the call told the family they were lucky; a few nights earlier, this same burglar had stabbed a home owner just five blocks away.

When youngsters return home to an empty house or apartment, it's a good idea to take steps to make the place look occupied. A light left on in the kitchen or bathroom, a radio playing, or lights on timers all help create the illusion that someone is home. A porch light left burning or set on a timer is a good idea if your children come home after dark.

Teach your children to be observant when they come home to an empty house. Does anything look suspicious? Is the door ajar? Are the draperies that were open this morning now closed? Is a window broken? Does it look like a door has been forced? Is there a strange car or a moving van in the driveway?

If anything looks unusual, instruct your children *not* to enter, but to go to a neighbor's home. In the past, children were instructed to phone their house to see if a family member had come home unexpectedly, then to alert the police. Now, most police departments want children to phone them immediately so they can respond quickly in case there is a burglary in progress. Emphasize to your children that they are not to enter the house until the police have checked it out. ***Make sure your children thoroughly understand these instructions.*** I am concerned with the youngsters in my classes who tell me they would sneak up to a window and peek in or barge right in and catch those bad guys. Some kids mistakenly think they're strong enough and tough enough to grapple with the bad guys. This false bravado is probably the result of heavy doses of television!

One of my students, Matthew, came home after school to find the front door of his home wide open. He remembered what I had told him to do in this situation, so he went to a neighbor and called the police, even though the neighbor tried to convince him to call his parents at work first. The police arrived, checked the house thoroughly, and found no sign of robbery or forced entry. Matthew was embarrassed to have bothered them for nothing, but the officers praised him for the way he handled the situation and gave him a special plastic police badge. The following day, they even called his elementary school principal and praised Matthew's actions. Matthew felt absolutely heroic! There's no guarantee every child will be treated that well, but it can happen!

Remind your children to lock the door behind them when they come home and to keep it locked. Also teach them to lock the door and take the keys with them if they go to a neighbor's house or just out to play with friends. Also teach them not to leave their key dangling in the lock, even if they are in a hurry to get the door open when they come home from school.

Children have a great fear of encountering a burglar in their home, even though statistics show it is not likely they will ever have to cope with this situation. Still, it is better for children to know what to do and never have to do it than to face such a situation unprepared. Remind your children to observe the house carefully before they enter. If they are already home and someone tries to break in, they have three choices:

1. The safest choice is to get out of the house and get help. The child can leave by another door or window and go to a neighbor's home to call the police.

2. If the child is unable to get out, he should quietly go to a secure room, lock the door, and phone the police from there. You should go through your home with your child and decide which room with a phone would be most secure. The master bedroom is often a good choice, since it usually has both a lock on the door and a phone.

3. If the child cannot get out of the house or phone the police, as a last resort, he should lock himself in the bathroom or hide in a closet or under a bed and be very quiet. If your inside doors cannot be locked, show your youngster how to prop a chair under the doorknob so the door can't be easily pushed open.

You may want to tell your youngsters if they should ever awaken to see someone strange in their bedroom, they should pretend to be asleep until the person leaves. Be sure to warn them that in the unlikely event they should encounter a burglar, they must do exactly as they are told to do. Reassure your youngsters that coming face to face with a burglar is a very rare occurrence and will probably never happen to them, but you want them to know what to do just in case. Most burglars deliberately plan their robbery for a time when they will not encounter people—even little people.

Caution your youngsters against trying to be heroes. I find little boys, especially, have an alarming tendency to be heroic. They boast they would use Dad's gun or get that burglar with a karate chop or sic the dog on him. Kids don't realize their strength would be almost useless against that of an adult, and if a child tried to use a weapon, it would almost certainly be taken from him and might even be used against him.

Dangerous Items at Home

Do you keep dangerous things like guns or illegal drugs in your home? Remember, when kids are home alone, they have free access to all areas of the house, and even when such things are kept under lock and key, there's always the chance that your children will find them. Cases of youngsters finding parents' drugs and using them are not uncommon, and stories of youngsters finding guns and shooting themselves or their friends are all too common. Don't let this happen at your house. If you don't want your kids to see it, use it, or try it, don't keep it at home.

Mark, a 10-year-old who attended our neighborhood school, was killed when he and a friend, home alone, found a gun his father had hidden in a box on the top shelf of the closet. The boys didn't think it was loaded, but the bullet hit Mark directly in the face. As the medics tried to save the boy, his father's anguished words were, "I thought I had hidden the gun." Mark was a really nice kid, a wonderful son, but like most kids his age, he was just curious about things hidden away.

It's a good idea to tell your children what to do if they encounter guns at a friend's house. They should not touch the gun and they should tell their friend to leave it alone. If the friend persists in playing with the weapon, your child should leave the house *immediately* and tell an adult what's happening. The child should *never* attempt to take the gun away from his friend.

Other Frightening Situations

In addition to handling phone calls, someone at the door, and potential burglaries, there are other frightening situations that can occur when youngsters are home alone. It is important for your children to know exactly how you expect them to deal with these possible problems.

Blackouts

During a power failure, part of your area may be temporarily blacked out. No matter how short a time the power may be off, such a situation can be terrifying to an unprepared child home alone. To prepare for a blackout, make sure a working flashlight is easily available. A magnetized one attached to the refrigerator is a good idea, since most kids can locate the refrigerator even in total darkness. Warn your youngsters not to use candles because of the fire danger. If the furnace goes off and the house gets cold, it is safer for youngsters to put on more clothing than to start a fire. If the power is off for longer than a few hours, children should not open the refrigerator or freezer more than absolutely necessary. Even without power, food will stay cold for some time if the door is kept closed.

Make sure your children realize that in most cases during a blackout, they will still be able to use the phone or hear it when it rings. However, if the storm that caused the blackout also downed the phone lines, phone service may be affected.

Set aside some games that your kids can play by flashlight, but caution them against reading ghost stories or telling fright-

ening tales. To pass the time, they could make a game of identifying everyday objects in the darkness by feel alone.

Severe Weather and Natural Disasters

While the chance of severe storms or natural disasters occurring
when parents are away is slim, if they *do* occur they can be terrifying and life-threatening to a child home alone. Usually these
phenomena happen with little warning. Phone lines are often
down, or jammed with calls, so parents aren't able to call home
to give instructions. Getting home from work can take much
longer than normal because of traffic delays. Unless they get help
from neighbors, youngsters home alone will have to fend for
themselves. They need to know what to do ahead of time.

You should discuss with your children the dangers of severe
weather or natural disasters in your particular area and what action you want them to take in the event that these things happen. You don't have to go into much detail about all the terrible
things that can happen; just give facts. It's a good idea for the
entire family to help assemble a severe weather–disaster kit that
can be kept easily accessible. Make sure all family members know
how to use the contents and understand the items are for emergency use only. The kit should contain:

> Portable battery-powered radio with extra batteries
>
> Flashlight with extra batteries
>
> Food that needs no refrigeration or cooking
>
> A first-aid kit
>
> Water stored in a clean plastic container
>
> Any other items your family thinks necessary, such as med-
> ication that's regularly taken

Find out which stations in your area broadcast storm and emergency information; write the station number on paper, and tape
it to the back of the radio for reference. Also decide on a meeting spot where family members should gather as soon as they
are able. Home is usually the logical meeting spot.

Winter Storms

During the winter, children are occasionally dismissed early from school when a severe storm is expected. Instruct your youngsters to go directly home if this happens and to stay inside until you get there. Also make sure they know you may be delayed in getting home because of the storm.

Thunderstorms

Thunder and lightning storms are one of the most common weather emergencies in most parts of the United States. If possible, children should try to get indoors during these storms. Teach them not to use the television, and to use the phone only in an emergency. If there is a lot of lightning, they should keep away from windows and outside doors. If they are caught outdoors and can't make it home, they should stay away from metal objects, open spaces, lone, tall trees, and hilltops. They should not lie flat on the ground, but should get down on all fours and crawl to a safer spot.

Tornadoes and Hurricanes

Usually there is advance warning before a tornado or hurricane, so parents have time to get home, but it's a good idea to tell your youngsters what to do just in case you aren't able to be with them. They should go immediately to the strongest part of the house, preferably the basement, if you have one, or a room without windows, such as a bathroom. They should stay there until they are sure the storm has passed. Make sure they understand about the calm in the eye of the storm and don't mistake that for the storm's end.

Flash Floods

Flash floods can be sudden and very violent, often with little advance warning. If your area is prone to such flooding, your children should know where to go to reach higher ground. Stress that they may not have time to rescue valuables or pets and that they must stay on higher ground until all danger has passed.

Severe Earthquakes

If you live in an earthquake-prone area, make sure your children know what to do if one should occur. In most cases, staying in the house or apartment is best. Instruct them to get under a heavy, solid piece of furniture, such as a desk or sturdy table, or to stand inside a door frame with feet and arms braced against the sides. After a quake subsides, children should avoid going outdoors because of downed electrical lines and broken gas mains. Youngsters should not use gas appliances until they have been checked out by the gas company. Make sure your children understand you may be delayed in getting home because of the quake.

Volcanic Eruptions

Until Mount Saint Helens blew its top in Washington State, volcanic eruptions were not thought to be a likely natural disaster in the United States. If you live near a potentially active volcano you might want to tell your children what to do in the event of a volcanic eruption or ash fall. If the sky gets very dark (darker than night) after an eruption, it probably means an ash cloud is approaching, and youngsters should get inside immediately and stay there. If they are caught out of doors, they should cover their mouth and nose with a cloth to avoid breathing in the ash and get inside as quickly as possible. Make sure they realize you will probably be delayed in traffic.

Blown Fuses

When too much electricity is used in one part of the house or an appliance malfunctions, a fuse may blow or a circuit breaker may trip. When this happens, electricity in that area of the house will go out. If this is a common occurrence in your home and you want your children to be able to handle such a situation, give them a lesson in changing the fuse or resetting the circuit breaker. If you have a breaker box, show them where the box is, which switches control which areas of the house, and how to reset them. Be sure each switch is labeled to show the part of your home it controls. If you have an older type box with fuses, caution your children against putting a penny behind a blown fuse.

If fuse or circuit problems happen regularly in your home or apartment, you should have the wiring checked by a professional. It may be necessary to upgrade the system to safeguard against fires.

Other Electrical Problems

Teach your children to respect electricity and handle it with care. Make sure they know they should never touch anything electric when their hands are wet because they may get a shock severe enough to kill them. We are all guilty of using hair dryers, curling irons, and razors in the bathroom near sinks and tubs full of water. This is an extremely dangerous practice and should be stopped, especially when we are trying to teach our children about electrical safety. Make it a family rule to keep all electrical appliances away from water.

If an electrical appliance malfunctions, tell your children not to try it again, but to leave it alone until a parent is home and can check it out.

Depending on your children's ages, you may want to teach them how to replace light bulbs that burn out when you are not home. Teach them to unplug or turn off the lamp or fixture before changing the bulb, and make sure they know never to put their fingers inside the bulb socket. Show them how to check the wattage number on the burned-out bulb, and emphasize the importance of replacing the bulb with one of the same number or lower. Tell them that if the wattage is higher, the bulb could get too hot and start a fire.

Leaking Water Pipes

It is important for everyone in the home to know where the main water shut-off valve is and how to operate it in case of an emergency. You should also tell your children how to deal with other individual water shut-offs, but generally it is a better idea to tell them to get adult help in the event of a major water leak.

Natural Gas Fumes

Natural gas is odorless, but gas utilities add an odor so a gas leak can be apparent by the smell. Your natural gas utility can often supply special scratch-and-sniff stickers so that your children will know what natural gas odor smells like. If kids come home and detect the strong odor of natural gas in the house, they should get out and stay out. They should call the fire department or the gas company from a neighbor's home. Make sure your children know the danger of an explosion if they light matches or any flame when gas fumes are present. In addition, they should not turn on or off any electrical switch, light, or appliance.

Activities for Practice

Here are some things to try with your children.

1. Take your children around the house to listen to the noises that the furnace, water heater, refrigerator, and other appliances make. This "tour" will make them less fearful when the furnace sounds like footfalls in the hall and the freezer moans.

2. Sometime when it's windy outdoors, make the house as quiet as possible so that you and your children can listen for house sounds the wind makes. Listen for branches that rub against the house and doors or windows that whistle or sigh when the wind blows. When your youngsters know exactly what those sounds really are, they will be less afraid.

3. Ask your local police department to conduct a security inspection of your home, pointing out any work that needs to be done to make it as burglar-proof as possible. Be sure to follow through on any recommendations they make.

4. If it is absolutely necessary for your children to accept deliveries, role-play the situation to see that they do so safely by first looking out the window to see if it is the person whom you are expecting. If that's not possible, when the person rings the bell or knocks, children should ask, "Who is it?" and only open the door when the person correctly identifies himself. Make sure your youngsters know not to ask, "Are you the repairperson we are expecting?"

5. Role play the following phone calls and situations with your child.

- A caller who asks for Mom or Dad
- A caller who asks for the child's address
- A wrong-number call in which the caller asks for the child's phone number
- An obscene call
- A prank call
- A threatening call
- A dead phone line
- A message for a family member

6. Ask your children what they would do if they were home alone and the following situations occurred.

- A blackout
- A blown fuse
- A broken pipe (*choose several different locations*)
- A strong odor of gas
- A thunderstorm (*away from home and at home*)
- A tornado or hurricane
- A flash flood
- An earthquake
- An ash fall after a volcanic eruption
- A severe winter storm
- Any other disasters or severe weather your area experiences

In Conclusion

When you leave your children home alone, it is vital that they know how to handle the situations that will arise—from the common everyday ones to the less likely life-threatening encounters. When kids have been told in advance exactly how you want them to handle a situation, they are more confident, far safer, and much more successful at taking care of themselves. This knowledge and confidence will help them conquer their fears when they're the ones in charge and will help them stay safe and sound when they're home alone.

Chapter 5

KEEPING CHILDREN SAFE
FROM FIRE

Lady bird, Lady bird
Fly away home.
Your house is on fire
Your children are alone!

Remember chanting that rhyme when you were a child? Did you ever stop to think of the implication of those words—"**Your house is on fire, your children are alone!**"? Now that we are adults with children of our own, those lines aren't funny; in fact they are downright terrifying—the stuff of nightmares.

We've all read those news reports: "Three children home alone, playing with matches. All three perished in the resulting house fire." "Five young children, left home alone at night, victims of a house fire." The very day I began writing this chapter, the newspapers carried stories about nine children dying in a Tacoma, Washington, house fire and four youngsters perishing in an Albany, Georgia, fire. All of them were home alone.

Big city fire departments report that as many as one out of every six emergency calls they receive involves children at home alone. The majority of children who die in fires do so at home alone. These numbers increase each year as more and more children are left by themselves. Parents must face the facts about the danger of fire and unsupervised youngsters and do all they can to make their children "fireproof."

Fire Prevention: A Family Affair

Statistics prove that families who have done what they can to make their homes fireproof and have practiced some basic fire drills have a much greater chance of surviving an actual fire than those families who leave things to chance. I know how little free time families have, but do plan to set aside one special evening for practicing fire safety. This one evening could be more important to you and your children than all the fire insurance you could carry!

Here are some suggestions for making this evening fun as well as interesting for the entire family.

1. Make a game, but a very serious game, of some of the activities.

2. Help your kids feel a sense of family responsibility. By participating in this fire drill they can help keep the rest of the family safe.

3. Emphasize that, just like the Scouts, one should always be prepared.

4. Tell the children that you are having fire drills and practice activities because they are so precious to you and you want to do everything possible to keep them safe.

Your family's fire safety evening should include the following activities.

1. Look for home fire hazards.

2. Practice using home fire equipment.

3. Conduct fire drills.

4. List fire safety rules.

5. Pretend to report a home fire.

Home Fire Hazards

Tell your children you are going to go through your home or apartment and surrounding outdoor areas looking for fire hazards, then pledge that all hazards found will be corrected immediately. In the case of something complicated like electrical wiring, pledge that you will arrange to have an expert handle it.

These are some common indoor fire hazards.

1. Frayed cords or loose wires on plugs.

2. Rugs covering electrical cords.

3. Overloaded electrical outlets.

4. Oily rags or flammable substances improperly stored. Because these substances can ignite spontaneously, they should be stored in airtight containers.

5. Paper or trash left lying around.

6. Furniture or curtains too close to a heat source such as a fireplace, wood stove, or electrical heater.

7. Matches or cigarette lighters within reach of youngsters. (This is one of the most common causes of home fires.)

8. Stove or oven used in an unsafe way.

9. Fireworks used or stored carelessly. Unused fireworks should be discarded rather than stored.

These are some common outdoor fire hazards.

1. Fireplace ashes cleaned out and left in bags, boxes, or cans near the house, garage, or breezeway or in an apartment hallway. Since ashes that were thought to be "dead" can ignite hours later, they should be stored in airtight metal containers.

2. Flammable liquids such as gasoline or kerosene stored improperly in outbuildings or yards. Such things should be in containers made for that purpose and stored out of children's reach.

3. Firepits, burning barrels, or incinerators too close to a building. Such devices should be at least 25 feet from any structure.

4. Open burning of leaves, garden debris, or trash during a dry season. Always secure a fire permit from your local fire department, have someone in constant attendance, and make sure water is readily available.

5. Careless use of fireworks. Make sure all fireworks are used carefully in safe areas under strict adult supervision.

Fire Equipment Demonstration

As your family is looking for fire hazards, be sure to point out your fire safety equipment: smoke alarms and fire extinguishers. If you don't already have these, be sure to buy them. These life-saving devices are inexpensive, and many insurance companies will give home owners a discount if the family has this equipment.

Smoke alarms or detectors should be installed on every floor of your home. If you are not sure of the best location, ask your local fire department for advice. If you smoke in bed, you should have a separate smoke alarm in your bedroom. Better yet, ***don't smoke in bed.***

If you have a battery-powered smoke detector, be sure to replace the batteries at least once a year or as often as necessary. Also make it a practice to test your smoke alarm at least once a month. Most models have a special test button you can push to sound an alarm; with others you must light a candle, blow it out, and hold the smoking wick near the unit to set off the alarm.

If you rent rather than own your home, you should know that in most areas the law says landlords must install smoke detectors in all units as well as supply fresh batteries as needed. Call your local fire department to see if this applies where you live.

If your smoke alarm goes off with every whiff of cooking or cigarette smoke, you may need to change its location, adjust the sensitivity, change worn-out batteries, or clean the unit. If that does not help, try replacing the detector with a model that is less sensitive. Do not simply remove the batteries; the lives of your family could depend on the early warning a smoke alarm gives.

Every home should also have at least one fire extinguisher. The one most commonly used in homes is a multipurpose dry chemical type that is effective against all three classes of fires:

Class A fires involving ordinary combustibles like wood, cloth, and paper

Class B fires involving flammable liquids, greases, gases, etc.

Class C fires involving live electrical equipment and appliances

Place the extinguisher where it is easily accessible to all family members. A kitchen is a good location since 65 percent of all house fires start there. It's a very good idea to have one in the kitchen and one in the basement or another part of the house. Most extinguishers come with a mounting bracket and should be permanently mounted on the bracket.

Make sure all family members know how to use the extinguisher. Often large extinguishers are too heavy for young children, so make sure yours can be handled by even the youngest member of your family who may be home alone. Check the extinguisher at least twice a year to make sure it is in good working order. Most extinguishers have a pressure dial that shows whether or not the unit needs to be refilled. Don't "practice" with your extinguisher, since it will have to be replaced or refilled if even a part of the contents is released.

Home Fire Drills

Fire drills are required at your youngsters' schools and perhaps even where you work. It's unfortunate they are not required in private homes.

With your children, practice how you would get out of your bedrooms if a fire broke out at night. Follow the steps for escaping a fire discussed later in this chapter. Have an alternate escape route, such as a window, in case you can't get out your bedroom door. Also practice escape routes from other rooms in your home. These drills will enable you to spot any problems you might encounter when you really need to escape. Some common problems are windows that have been painted shut or are difficult to open, screens or bars that cannot be removed from windows, and long drops to the ground. If you live in an apartment building, see page 52 for additional instructions for escaping from apartment fires.

Part of the fire drill should be spent deciding on where family members will gather once they have escaped from a house fire. It is vital to have a specific meeting place so that it can easily be determined if all family members are out of the house. Some common meeting places are the street in front of your home or apartment, the mailbox, or a neighbor's yard. Make sure all family members know the exact location and the importance of immediately gathering at that spot to be accounted for.

Family Fire Safety Rules

Make a list of fire safety rules for your family to follow. Here are some of the most common ones.

1. Children should *never* play with matches, fireworks, candles, kerosene, gasoline, or any flammable substances. (Unsupervised children are often strongly tempted to experiment with these dangerous things, so this rule should be emphasized.)

2. Generally, children under 12 should not use the stove or oven. If you do allow your older children to use the stove, they should make sure any long hair is tied back and that they do not wear clothing with loose flowing sleeves that could drape over a hot burner and catch fire. Also caution them to keep pan handles turned toward the back of the stove so the pans in use won't be accidentally knocked off. Warn your children to be especially careful not to spill hot liquids on themselves or others.

3. Don't plug too many appliances into one outlet at the same time, since overloaded outlets can cause fires. Only use as many appliances at one time as the outlet has plugs for.

4. Sleep with bedroom doors closed. Should a fire break out while your family is asleep, closed doors will keep out smoke and fire and give you extra time to escape through a window. An alternative to keeping doors closed is to install a smoke alarm or alarms in the hall near the bedrooms.

If your children balk at closing their bedroom doors at night, it's often because they like the security a hall light provides. You can solve this difficulty by putting a small night-light inside their rooms. To save their feelings, tell them the light is there so you can see when you come in to check on them, not because they need it.

Reporting a Fire

Make sure everyone in your family knows the fire department phone number by heart. It is also a good idea if both you and your neighbors have this and other emergency numbers posted on or beside the phones. Memorized numbers can be forgotten during extreme stress; so can your own address even though you have lived there for years. Emergency dispatchers can relate many stories of adults whose minds went blank during a crisis. So list your address, too. (There is a form for this purpose in the Appendix.)

Emphasize that, during a fire, family members should first holler to alert others, then get out of the house and go to the designated meeting spot. Only then should they report the fire from a neighbor's phone. No one should attempt to call the fire department from within a burning house. If your neighbors are not conveniently nearby or don't have a phone, locate the nearest firebox and show your children how to use it.

Make sure your children speak slowly and loudly when they practice reporting a fire. They will need to tell the dispatcher the complete street address and the nearest cross street. Although the dispatchers who answer such calls send the fire equipment out as soon as they receive the call, they often keep the caller on the line to get any further information which can be relayed by radio to the fire trucks en route. Because of this, it is important to stay on the line until you are told to hang up.

Step-by-Step Escape from a House Fire

Parents must emphasize, over and over, that the only priceless and irreplaceable things in a house are the *people*. Furniture, silver, jewelry, heirlooms, and even family pets can be replaced. It is also vital that children realize they must not do anything that delays their getting out as quickly as possible. They must not get dressed, stop to gather up any possessions whatsoever, or rescue pets that are beyond their immediate reach.

A fireman told me about a youngster who died in a house fire. The child was still clutching his mother's jewelry box when his body was carried from the house. Once in jest, the boy's mother had talked about saving the family jewels if there was ever a fire. The mother was only joking. Naturally she valued her son's life far more than any jewelry, but parents need to make that very, very clear to their children.

Parents must also make absolutely sure their youngsters know that they should never try to hide from a house fire. Most firemen can tell tragic stories of finding children's bodies under beds and in closets, where they perished while trying to hide from a fire. Tell your kids that even if they started the fire themselves, they must get out, *not hide*.

Step 1: Alert Others

Awakening or alerting other family members to the danger is the first step when someone hears a smoke alarm, smells smoke, or thinks there is a fire in the house. Screaming, pounding on the walls, and hollering are all effective.

Step 2: Test Doors for Heat

If a fire occurs when the family is asleep (remember to sleep with bedroom doors closed), first feel the closed door with the palm of your hand to see if it is hot before you open it. If it feels hot or if there is smoke seeping under the door, **keep the door closed.** Most wooden interior doors will hold back a fire for at least ten minutes, but if you open the door, the flames or smoke may surge into the room.

If the door feels hot, you will have to find another way to get out of the room. Stuff clothing or bedding around the cracks of the door, then try to escape through a window. All family members should know in advance how to open windows and remove window screens. If a window cannot be opened, use a dresser drawer or any other handy object to break the glass. To keep from getting cut by small pieces of glass that remain in the window frame, cover the jagged edges with a blanket, rug, or bedspread, then climb through the opening. If you cannot jump down from the window, scream for help and wait to be rescued. If your bedrooms are on an upper floor, you can purchase collapsible fire safety ladders and learn how to use them or else make some other provisions for getting down.

If the door doesn't feel hot, brace your foot against it and first open it just a few inches to see if it's safe to escape through the hall or out through another part of the house. If there is smoke, get down and crawl on the floor, since the freshest air is just a few inches above the floor.

Step 3: Family Meeting Spot

After escaping from the fire, all family members should go directly to the prearranged meeting place and stay there until everyone is accounted for. This meeting place should be known to everyone, and not changed from time to time.

If, after reporting to your meeting place, you discover someone may still be trapped inside the house, never let your children go back in. Even an adult should seriously evaluate the dangers of trying to rescue someone and getting back out safely. It is almost always better to wait until the fire department arrives and let them attempt the rescue, since they have the equipment and the training.

Step 4: Reporting a Fire

After, and *only* after, your family is out of the house and has gathered at the meeting place, should someone go to the closest neighbor or firebox to call the fire department.

Escaping from an Apartment Fire

Instructions for escaping from an apartment fire differ from instructions for single-family home dwellers.

As soon as you move into a building, take some time to locate alarms and any other emergency fire equipment. If there are no fire alarms, ask your landlord to install one on each floor. Some cities also require landlords to install emergency battery-operated lights in the hallways. Your local fire department will know about the regulations in your area.

If you suspect there is a fire in your apartment building, it is important to alert not only family members but other tenants as well, if at all possible. Remember to feel your own door to the common hallway. Do not open it if it's hot. If it feels cool and you believe you can safely open it, use the alarms or fireboxes in the hallway to alert others. If time permits, bang on unit doors and holler "Fire!" then get out of the building.

When leaving the building, close the door to your unit, but do not lock it because fire fighters may need to get in if the fire is in your apartment. Also, if you are unable to get out of the building, you may have to go back into your unit or another unit further from the fire. If you have to go back or are unable to go out into the hall because of heavy smoke or flames, stuff wet clothing, towels, or blankets in the cracks under and around the door, then open or break out a window, holler to attract attention, and wait to be rescued. A sheet or blanket draped from your window will help draw attention to your location.

When escaping from an apartment fire, always use the stairs. If the smoke in the stairwell is too thick to permit escape, go back to your apartment. ***Never use the elevator during a fire.*** The updraft in an elevator shaft may suck up the flames and smoke or the elevator may stop, trapping you. Some newer elevators may be programmed to automatically sink to the lobby floor in an emergency, but that updraft effect may make them unsafe, too.

If Clothing Catches on Fire

When a child's clothing catches fire, often his or her first response is to panic and run. Since this action fans the flames and makes them burn faster, it's important to teach your children to ***stop, drop, and roll:*** *stop* where they are, *drop* to the ground and cover their face with their hands, and *roll* back and forth to smother the flames. Any nearby blankets, tarps, or rugs can also be used to smother the flames. When the fire is out, the child should get medical attention as quickly as possible.

If someone else's clothing catches fire, tell your youngsters to follow the same procedure: stop or grab the person, throw him to the ground, and then roll him back and forth to smother the fire. Again, a rug or blanket can be used to help smother the flames. When the fire is out, get medical help for the victim.

Since it's difficult for children to imagine how easily flames can be smothered, it's a good idea for parents to demonstrate.

Take a frying pan outdoors, put some paper or cloth in the pan and light it, then use either a pan lid, a heavy cloth, a folded newspaper, or a magazine to smother the flames. Then light the fire again and have your child smother the flames.

Putting Out Small Household Fires

Generally when children are home alone and a fire breaks out, the best policy is for them to get out and get help; however, there are some small household fires that most children can put out themselves. As a parent, you will have to set the policy in your household by determining your children's maturity and ability to handle a crisis situation. If you tell your children they may attempt to put out small household fires, also tell them if they have *any doubts whatsoever,* they should not try to be heroic, but should get out and turn in an alarm.

The following questions will help determine whether or not youngsters should try to extinguish a small fire.

1. Do they have a way to get out if they fight the fire and it gets larger, or would they be trapped? For example, if a small fire starts near the bottom of the basement stairs, the child may not be able to escape up the stairs if the fire spreads.

2. Can they contain the fire in the room by shutting the door if they are unsuccessful in extinguishing it? A fire in a bathroom can be more readily closed off from the rest of the house than a fire in an open living room.

3. Is there a fire extinguisher or water handy to put out the fire?

4. Will fighting the fire, instead of getting out, put the lives of others in danger? Your children should not waste precious time fighting a fire if there is a baby or a bedridden adult in the house who will need help escaping from the fire.

If you think your children are capable of trying to put out a small fire, instruct them in dealing with the following common house fires.

GREASE FIRES

Tell your children that a small grease fire in a pan on the stove can usually be extinguished by putting the lid on the pan and turning off the burner. Without air, the fire will go out. If baking *soda* is handy, it can be thrown on a grease fire to smother the flames. Make sure your children know where it is kept, and make sure they do not confuse it with baking *powder* or anything else. Flour, sugar, or baking powder should never be used in place of baking soda; they may "explode" and spread the fire. An all-purpose fire extinguisher can also be used on a grease fire. Teach your children they must never throw water on a grease fire, as that will scatter the fire and make it worse. They must never try to carry a pan of burning grease, since it can easily spill and burn them or spread the fire. If they can't quickly put out a grease fire, they should get out and call the fire department. In general, children under 12 should not even attempt to put out a grease fire, but most parents of youngsters home alone think it is not safe for children under 12 to be using the stove anyway.

Sometimes burned food or grease that has spilled into the reflector pans below the burner catches fire. This can usually be extinguished by turning off the burner and putting a lid over it until the flame goes out. Essentially, this prevents air from getting to the fire, thus smothering the flames.

OVEN FIRES

Fires in the oven usually go out by themselves when the heat is turned off and the oven door is closed to cut off the oxygen supply. Tell your youngsters that if this doesn't work, they should use a fire extinguisher or throw baking soda on the flames.

SMALL FIRES IN CONTAINERS

Fires in containers such as a metal wastebasket can often be put out by covering the container to shut off the air. A metal cookie sheet, large frying pan, or even a heavy rug can be used. Generally children over 9 can put out this type of fire by smothering it or using a fire extinguisher. If a fire occurs in a plastic or raffia wastebasket, a fire extinguisher should be used.

ELECTRICAL APPLIANCE FIRES

Tell your children that if an electrical appliance smokes or catches fire, they should try to unplug it if they can. *After* it has been unplugged, and *only* after it has been unplugged, if necessary the fire can be extinguished with water. Make sure children understand they should **never throw water on an appliance that is still plugged in.** That could result in a serious or even fatal electrical shock. If the appliance cannot be unplugged, a multipurpose fire extinguisher can be used.

TELEVISION FIRES

Tell your youngsters if they ever see smoke or sparks coming from the television, or hear a crackling sound inside the set, they should unplug it. If that is not possible, they should stay well away from the set and call the fire department. A television on fire *could* explode. Also remind your family to keep coffee, soda pop, and the like off the top of the television set because liquids spilled down inside a TV can cause a fire.

Child Arsonists

Although many youngsters go through a stage of being interested in fire, most children quickly realize how dangerous it is and stop. Some troubled youngsters never get over playing with fire and become what fire departments term a "child fire setter" or "child arsonist."

Most of these youngsters have at least some of the following characteristics: They often come from a home where parents have divorced. They may be abused or neglected children who don't fit in with their peer group. Often they are poor students, feel a deep hatred toward a family member, are chronic bed wetters, and are cruel to animals. If a child does not outgrow his experimentation with fire and has some of those characteristics, the situation should be considered potentially dangerous. Parents should seek immediate professional help for the troubled child.

Parents who suspect their child is abnormally interested in fire or know the youngster has set a fire should *never* leave that child unsupervised. The child should always be cared for by a responsible baby-sitter, or some kind of alternative arrangement should be made until the parents are positive the child can be trusted not to play with fire when home alone. If one of your children's friends seems abnormally interested in fire, do that youngster a favor by telling the child's parents if they are not already aware of it. *Never* allow that child in your home unless he is carefully supervised. Be sure your children also know that the child is not to be allowed in your house.

Activities for Practice

Critical Fire Situations

1. Ask your kids to show you what they would do if their jeans were on fire.

2. Ask your youngsters to demonstrate what they would do if a friend's clothing caught on fire and the friend panicked and ran.

3. Ask your children what they would do if they were escaping from a fire and suddenly remembered that a valuable family coin collection was still inside the burning house.

4. Ask your children to pretend they are escaping from a house fire when they hear their dog and her puppies crying and barking at the other end of the house near the fire. Should they attempt to rescue the animals?

Fire Drill Practice

Go into your children's bedrooms. Tell them to close the door, hop in bed, cover up, and pretend they are asleep. Now make a "Yeeeep" noise to indicate the smoke alarm. Have your kids show what they would do when they hear the alarm. Have them pretend the door is cool and see if they know what to do. Then pretend the door is hot and see how they react. Ask them to open their window, then pretend the window is stuck, and see if they know what to do. If they forget some of the steps, refer to the instructions in this chapter.

Reporting a Fire

Have your children practice reporting a fire at your house by calling from a neighbor's phone instead of phoning from home. Make sure your kids can properly report your address as well as the closest cross street. Make them repeat the information if they give it too quickly or too quietly. Emphasize that they must speak clearly (even loudly) and slowly. At the end of this session, remind your children that under no circumstances should they call an emergency phone number just for practice or as a joke. People can be prosecuted for causing false alarms.

Putting Out Small Household Fires

Pretend that your child comes home from school and finds the iron left on and the ironing board smoldering. Given your home layout and location of your fire extinguisher, ask your child what he would do.

Pretend your youngsters are old enough to fry chicken on the stove. Ask them what they would do if the pan grease ignited.

Pretend you were heating a pizza in the oven, then went to the neighbors for a minute and left your kids home alone. The melting cheese ran over the pan and caught fire in the oven. Ask your child what she would do.

Pretend your children are home alone when the TV makes a crackling noise, the picture goes dark, and the set begins to smoke. Ask them what they would do.

In Conclusion

Home fires are extreme emergencies where knowledge, practice, and previous planning will, in large part, determine the outcome. We all hope and pray that our children will never experience a house fire; however, should a fire occur when your youngsters are home alone, the instructions and exercises in this chapter will help keep your most precious possessions—your children—safe and sound.

Chapter 6

KIDS IN THE KITCHEN

Remember when you were a kid? Probably your mom stayed home in those days and you spent a lot of time with her in the kitchen, not only becoming familiar with the appliances, but soaking up a great deal of knowledge about cooking. Now most of us are working full-time while raising our children, so we don't always have time to spend in the kitchen. With the new reliance on fast foods and frozen dinners, many of us have pangs of guilt and regret not only because our offspring are unfamiliar with our kitchens but because both boys and girls are missing out on some of the joys of cooking.

We don't have to give up jobs or curtail promising careers to teach our kids about the kitchen, but we busy parents will have to put forth an extra effort to teach our "home-alone" youngsters how to work in the kitchen with safety, skill, and confidence.

When you teach your youngsters about cooking and using kitchen appliances, the kids will have more fun, learn more, and feel closer to you if you adopt the role of fellow explorer and avoid the one of know-it-all adult. The know-it-all adult sternly commands, "Use only dishwasher soap in the dishwasher!" while the fellow explorer asks, "Why is it important to use only dishwasher soap and not any other kind in the dishwasher? What would happen if we used laundry detergent?" Admittedly, the fellow explorer spends more time answering questions and giving explanations, but children learn more from this style. Some parents worry that the fellow explorer approach will give the youngsters ideas for further experimentation when they are alone. The reverse is true; most children aren't malicious, just curious. If they know the reason why they shouldn't do things, they aren't as likely to try them. Fellow explorers also have better communication with children than know-it-all adults.

Food for Kids:
Nutritious, Tasty, and Supersimple

Commonsense Nutrition

It's a good idea for you and your children to spend some time going over the four main food groups so that they understand why it's important for growing youngsters to eat a balanced diet and avoid too much junk food. You don't have to demonstrate that good food affects health with your own live mice, but you can tell this story of a teacher who did.

MICE ON A DIET

A teacher brought eight mice to her classroom and separated them into two cages. One group of four was fed a so-called junk-food diet, while the other four dined on well-balanced mouse meals.

After just one week the class could see that the junk-food eaters wobbled when they walked; their fur was dull and they slept most of the time. As the teacher had predicted, the mice on the balanced diet appeared to be in the peak of rodent health.

Even though both groups of mice were then fed good diets, the mice that originally had the deficient diet never completely regained their health and were always smaller and slower than the others. It wasn't hard for the class to conclude that proper diet is very important for both mice and children!

Emphasize to your children that healthy eating and common-sense nutrition can be a simple matter of choosing a variety of foods each day from the four main food groups. Before their teen years, children should have daily helpings of at least two servings from the meat and protein group, four servings from the fruit and vegetable group, four from the grain and cereal group, and three from the milk and dairy-products group.

The four food groups are:

Meat and Protein – This group includes meat, fish and other seafood, eggs, poultry, nuts, and beans.

Fruit and Vegetable – This group includes fruit (apples, bananas, oranges, etc.) and vegetables (spinach, carrots, squash, green beans, peas, corn, etc.).

Grain and Cereal – This group includes pastas, such as macaroni and spaghetti; rice; and grain products, such as breads, rolls, muffins, and so forth.

Milk and Dairy Products – This group includes milk and dairy products such as cheese, yogurt, and butter.

Sometimes a fifth group, which includes fats and sugars, is added to this list. Some fats are necessary in our diet, but it's a good idea to teach your children to avoid too much of this so-called junk food, such as candy bars, cookies high in sugar, and the like.

Is the Cupboard Bare?

Some youngsters have a hard time finding anything good to eat when they're home alone; like Old Mother Hubbard, their cupboard is bare. One child I know complained to her Dad that there was nothing to eat. He told her to look in the cupboard because there was plenty of food. To prove her point, the girl made a list of the cupboard's contents and presented it to her father. Here's the list:

Bouillon soup

Canned creamed corn

Tomato paste

A box of Jell-O

Wheat germ

Dried barley

Egg noodles

Water chestnuts

Old-fashioned rolled oats

Pickled beets

Kippered herring

Instant coffee

The list got the father's attention and he took his daughter grocery shopping. Parents are wise to remember this when assuming the cupboards are full: most children simply don't know what to do with water chestnuts, pickled beets, kippered herring, and egg noodles, yet they get along quite nicely with fruit, peanut butter, jelly, bread, cereal, and milk.

Snack Ideas

After-school snacks are the most common "meal" prepared by youngsters. Since most children are simply starving when they get home from school, snacks need to be quick and easy. Here are some suggestions:

Yogurt

Fresh fruit

Peanut butter with almost anything on almost anything

Jelly or jam on almost anything

Cookies, either store-bought or homemade

Fresh vegetables already cut and peeled

Cheese

Milk

Give some consideration to your children's likes and dislikes. If they detest unpeeled apples, leave fruits such as bananas or plums as a snack. Fresh strawberries may be a special treat. Children who don't like plain yogurt may be won over by fruit-flavored yogurt. Or make up their favorite flavor of Jell-O with fruit in individual bowls to provide a handy and quick snack. If your child likes juice, occasionally suggest it as a substitute for fruit, but be sure the juice you buy is the real thing, not the less nutritious fruitades or drinks, which are mostly flavored sugar water. Dried fruits and commercial or homemade fruit leathers made from fruit purees are tasty and nutritious. Pudding can be bought in individual serving cans, or youngsters can make the instant packaged kind.

If you have not been successful in convincing your children to eat raw vegetables, you may discover their disinterest is actually laziness. Left unprepared in the refrigerator, most vegetables will hang around until they are long dead, passed over in favor of more easily prepared snacks; but if you spend a little time peeling and cutting those same vegetables, they are usually devoured.

Breakfast Ideas

Make sure your children know the importance of eating a good breakfast. The word "breakfast" itself gives a clue. This first meal of the day breaks the fast from the last meal of the previous evening. Breakfast provides the fuel the body needs to begin a whole new day. Numerous studies have proven that children who skip breakfast often don't think or play well; they usually have a poorer attitude, tire more easily, and aren't as efficient as students who eat a nourishing breakfast.

A good breakfast should have choices from three different food groups, but need not be the traditional fare. Encourage your youngsters to try some of these sample meals:

Cold cereal, fruit juice, and a glass of milk

Packaged instant hot cereal (made with hot tap water), fruit, and milk

Toast with cheese, milk, fruit or fruit juice

Peanut butter and jelly sandwich, fruit, and milk

Tuna sandwich, fruit or juice, and milk

Lunch Ideas

If your children make their own school lunch, make sure you have nutritious fixings around, and encourage them to include something from the four food groups. The milk which many youngsters buy at school is considered a food group. It's pretty common for students to trade foods at lunchtime, so be sure your children know they should still try to eat a balanced lunch, even if the makings come from a friend.

During vacations or other days at home, children are usually responsible for fixing their own lunches. Sandwiches seem to be standard fare and, combined with fruit and a glass of milk, make a nutritious meal. If you allow your youngsters to use the stove, oven, or microwave, lunches can be expanded to include easy-to-fix canned soups, frozen meat dishes, and other such products.

Dinner Ideas

Parents are usually responsible for the evening meal, but it's a good idea to have something in reserve in case you are delayed and children must make their own dinner. This is when TV dinners come in handy. If your youngsters use the microwave oven, make sure they understand the food must always be removed from foil containers and placed on microwave-safe dishes. Some parents make sure they buy only dinners in microwave-safe containers. Also go over the other rules for microwave use discussed on page 71. If you think your children are too young to use the stove, microwave, or toaster oven, be sure you always have the ingredients on hand for the old standby—peanut butter and jelly sandwiches. Along with fruit or vegetables and milk, this can occasionally pass for dinner.

Getting the Kids to Cook Dinner

If your youngsters are old enough to use the stove (usually age 12 and above), try some of these strategies to make cooking dinner a fun opportunity rather than a chore. Kids may love a "special opportunity," but we all know how they feel about chores!

One family in our neighborhood pays the children to prepare dinner one or two nights a week. The cook is paid $2.50

per dinner and the table setter and cleanup person is paid $1.50. Both parents think this is cheaper than going to a fast-food restaurant or buying expensive prepared foods. The youngsters have also learned to feel competent in the kitchen.

Another family has taught each child to prepare a complete meal. One child can make a wonderful Mandarin chicken dinner, another can fix fantastic tostadas, and the third youngster specializes in spaghetti. The youngsters take turns fixing complete meals when their busy parents have to declare an emergency.

In another family, one child exhibits great cooking potential and wants to be the chef every time. The other child doesn't care about cooking and is content to set the table and clean up. Of course this is unusual, but you may be successful in getting your children to take turns at these chores.

After I bought a simple, colorfully illustrated children's cookbook, my own daughters vied to be the very first to try out the recipes and took turns cooking dinner each night for a week. Naturally that didn't last, but I find that our library has a large supply of children's cookbooks and each time I bring one home, it seems to restimulate their cooking interest. If you try this, take care to pick the right cookbook for your child's age group. Complicated cookbooks that call for ingredients not readily available in normal households can easily discourage a child.

Dangers in the Kitchen

The kitchen can also be one of the most dangerous rooms in your entire house. It's the site of a very high percentage of household accidents. Since most youngsters spend a lot of time in the kitchen, make sure they are aware of these dangers.

Stoves and Ovens

As a conservative guideline, youngsters under the age of 12 should not be allowed to use the stove or oven when they're home alone. If you think your child is old enough and careful enough to use these appliances, take the time to give complete instructions on their use, have practice sessions together, and go over the rules and instructions again after the youngster has used the appliances for a few weeks.

If you do not want your children to use the stove or oven, explain why. Explain that even adults sometimes go off and leave something cooking or forget to turn off a burner. It's just too easy for kids to forget what's cooking and go off to play, leaving the food to burn, ruining the pan, or possibly even starting a fire.

Many working parents invest in microwave ovens. Speedy cooking is the main advantage, but microwaves are safer than conventional ovens because there is little heat produced and the oven goes off by itself even if the user has skipped off to swing or shoot a few baskets. If you allow your children to use the microwave, make sure they observe the precautions listed on page 71.

Sharp Kitchen Tools

Teach your children the safe way to cut, chop, grate, and peel. If they learn correctly right from the start, they will have fewer accidents. It's a good idea to put kids' kitchen tools (knives that will do the job, but aren't too sharp) in a special place for children's use. Encourage your youngsters to cut on a cutting board, not the counter.

Demonstrate the proper way to use a knife. Let your young ones practice holding the food on a cutting board with their left hand while they cut down through the food onto the board with their right hand. Apples, celery, and potatoes are easy foods for children to practice on.

Also demonstrate the correct way to use a potato peeler, that is, away from the body. Let your youngsters practice on potatoes or apples until they become proficient.

It's also a good idea to show your children how to use a grater to shred cheese or cabbage. See that they are careful not to get fingers too close to the sharp surface.

No Mountain Climbing

Forbid mountain climbing in your kitchen; no climbing on counters, using drawers for steps, or swinging from cupboard doors. If commonly used items in your kitchen are out of a child's reach, make sure a sturdy stool or chair is available, or consider placing these things in a lower cupboard.

Spills and Broken Glass

Some youngsters think cleaning up a spill means letting the dog or cat lick the floor, but most spills need a little more than a quick once-over. Spills usually need the full treatment—wash with soap and water and let dry—or the floor may stay sticky or dangerously slippery. Taking a spill on a spill may sound funny, but serious injuries can result. Parents can help by keeping paper towels, rags, mops, brooms, dustpans, and other cleanup supplies within children's reach.

All children drop and break things, so it's important to teach them how to clean up broken glass. They should first pick up and dispose of the large pieces, being careful not to get cut, then sweep the other pieces into a dustpan. Ideally, the whole area should then be gone over with thick layers of damp paper towels to pick up any tiny glass slivers that may remain. It is not a good idea to vacuum up broken glass, since the sharp glass could damage the machine.

Ask your children to let you know when they have broken something, not because you will be mad, but because you want to make sure it was cleaned up safely and completely. Family members should also be told if there is glass in a wastebasket or garbage pail so that they won't stomp down on the trash and get cut. Try to be understanding when things get broken; most plates and glasses can easily be replaced, but children's self-esteem is fragile and difficult to restore.

A Shocking Experience

Children should never have to learn about the dangers of electric shocks by experience! Make sure they know that when water and electricity get together, a dangerous or even deadly shock can be produced. Make sure your children know these basic rules about electrical appliances.

1. *Never* touch any electrical appliance with wet hands or if you are standing in water.

2. *Never* use an electrical appliance near water: If the appliance should contact the water, the user could be electrocuted.

3. *Always* hold the rubber base of a plug when inserting it into an electrical outlet. Don't let your fingers touch the metal prongs of the plug. When removing a plug, you should always grip the base firmly and pull; don't remove the plug by pulling on the cord.

4. *Never* throw water on an appliance that is still plugged in. After the appliance is unplugged, water can be used. If the appliance cannot be unplugged, use an all-purpose fire extinguisher.

5. If an appliance is not working properly, turn it off, unplug it, and don't use it again until an adult has thoroughly checked it out.

Wildlife in the Refrigerator

If your family is like most, refrigerated leftovers are occasionally overlooked until colonies of mold beg for attention or until you must either search for the offending stinker or evacuate the house!

Since some youngsters will eat just about anything, it's important to educate your offspring about molds. You don't have to go into botanical details, but do emphasize that mold on food means "Do not eat whatever this was!" If food looks bad, smells bad, or is at all questionable, kids should leave it alone.

Suspicious Canned Goods

If a can bulges, shows signs of leaking, or hisses abnormally when opened, it may mean the food inside is spoiled and should not be used. Although rare in commercially canned foods, botulism is deadly. A good family motto might be, "When in doubt, dump it out!"

One of my girls threw away two cans of green beans because they hissed when she opened them and she thought they might be spoiled. Later on when I opened a can, she heard it hiss too and asked why. After I explained how vacuum-packed cans make a noise when the lid is pierced and pressure released, she said her cans had hissed the same way and were probably perfectly all right when she threw them out. We praised her anyway for not taking chances. Although parents want children to know their safety is far more important than the price of green beans, it's a good idea to teach your children to recognize the normal hiss of a vacuum-packed can.

Kitchen Appliances

Here is a conservative guideline to help you decide when your youngsters are old enough to use certain kitchen appliances. This guideline is based on interviews with hundreds of working and nonworking parents and their children. Of course, you must consider your own child's ability and sense of responsibility.

Appliance	Under 12	12 to 16 years	16 to adult
Blender	x		
Dishwasher	x		
Electric can opener	x		
Garbage disposal		x	
Microwave oven	x		
Mixer		x	
Stove or oven		x	
Toasters and toaster oven	x		
Trash compactor			x

If you make the decision to let your children use kitchen appliances, give them a detailed demonstration of how the appliances work. To make sure that nothing goes wrong, also write out instructions or compile a checklist for your youngsters to follow. When you demonstrate how the appliances work, be sure to include the following information.

- Exactly how to use the appliance
- What not to do
- Dangers of that particular appliance

- How to clean it
- Any special quirks or peculiar tricks of the appliance and how to cope with them

If you decide a certain appliance is off limits without adult supervision, be sure your children are clearly aware they are not to use that appliance. Be sure to tell them your reasons. If you have the following appliances, include them in your kitchen tour.

Blender

- Your children should know the elementary fact that the blender top must be on securely or food will splatter.
- Caution children not to put a spoon or similar utensil in the blender until it has been turned off and the blades stop. As added insurance, the blender can also be unplugged. They should be sure the utensil is removed before restarting the blender.
- If ice is to be added to the blender, the cubes should be put in slowly, one at a time, to avoid damaging the blades or breaking the container.

Dishwasher

- Show your child how to rinse and load the dishes, put in the dishwasher detergent, and start the machine.
- Warn youngsters to be careful that things don't fall down onto the heating element in the bottom of the dishwasher, where they can burn. If something does fall, it should be retrieved before starting the machine.
- Stress that only special dishwasher detergent should be used because any other soap can flood the kitchen with suds.
- Make sure your child can tell the difference between the normal steam coming from the dishwasher and smoke that might indicate something is on fire. Explain that normal steam rising from the machine feels damp and dissipates rapidly, while smoke is more visible and smells like something burning. Warn them that steam

from the unit can burn them if they open the door too quickly.

- If the youngster suspects a fire, the machine should be turned off and the door left closed.

Electric Can Opener

- Show youngsters how to use the electric can opener.
- Caution them not to leave the sharp lid attached to the unit but to carefully remove and throw it away.
- If certain cans are too large or heavy for the opener, instruct your child to use a hand-held can opener.

Garbage Disposal

- Your youngsters should know that when they turn on the disposal, the cold water should also be turned on.
- Emphasize that hands must never be put down in the garbage disposal when it is operating. If something that does not belong there has fallen in, the disposal should be turned off. When it comes to a complete stop, then the item can be retrieved. Better yet, tell your kids to make sure silverware or nonfood items aren't left where they could possibly fall in, become damaged, and possibly break the disposal.

Microwave Oven

- Your youngsters should know how to correctly operate the microwave oven. They should realize that it is not a toy to play or experiment with.
- Caution them never to put anything metal (with metal edges or decorations) in the oven as this may damage the unit.
- They should never attempt to operate the microwave with the door open, since this can result in their exposure to harmful microwave energy. The oven should also not be run when it is empty.

- If food is overcooked and catches fire, they should stop the microwave oven and leave the door closed. Cut off from the oxygen supply, the fire will soon go out. They should not open the door until the fire is completely out.

- Tell your children they must never put any living thing (cat, bird, mouse, turtle, etc.) in the microwave oven. Although it is hard to imagine anyone doing this, it has happened and the animal has been killed.

- Warn youngsters not to use the unit if they suspect it is broken. An adult should check it out first.

Mixer

- Caution youngsters not to put fingers in or near the beaters, and make sure the mixer is completely stopped before using a spoon in the mixing bowl.

- If the beaters labor too hard to mix something, it is better to mix it by hand.

Stove or Oven

- Caution your children to double-check to be sure the oven or stove is always turned off after being used. It is so easy to forget and leave it on.

- Teach children to use potholders to move hot dishes or pans.

- Make it a family habit to turn pan handles toward the rear of the stove so that they won't be knocked off accidentally.

- Your children should always tie back long hair and avoid wearing shirts or blouses with long, flowing sleeves that could catch fire when cooking.

- If you want your children to be able to relight the pilot light on your stove or light the gas in an oven, teach them how.

Toaster and Toaster Oven

- If the bread gets stuck in the toaster, make sure your children know they can get a nasty shock if they don't unplug the toaster before trying to get the bread out.

- When children use a toaster oven, they should make sure the unit is turned off after use.

Trash Compactor

- Warn children the compactor is not a toy and can be very dangerous if not used correctly.

- If you want to keep odors from building up, ask your children to rinse cans and bottles before discarding them.

- Teach them how to wrap glass bottles in newspaper to keep the broken glass from being a hazard.

- It is probably all right for children to throw trash into the unit, but it is safest if only adults activate the compactor.

Put these rules and suggestions into your own words. Confess to any blunders or accidents you've had while operating kitchen appliances. Children love to know their parents did some dumb things and aren't afraid to admit it; it shows that parents are human, too.

Cleaning Up Kitchen Messes

Most parents complain that their young ones leave the kitchen in a horrible mess—dirty plates and glasses, sticky counters, spilled food, and food left out of the refrigerator. If this is a problem at your house, make it a definite rule that the kitchen must be cleaned up after use or it is not to be used at all. Give a first warning and make the culprit help clean up. The second warning should involve a penalty of some sort (such as unloading the dishwasher an extra time), and the third infraction should mean the end of kitchen privileges for a period of time or banning the child from a family activity, such as going out to dinner with the rest of the family the next time you eat out. To help kids keep the kitchen clean, some parents think the convenience of providing paper plates and cups outweighs the added expense.

Activities for Practice

1. Ask your children how they would get a jar of peanut butter that was stored on the top shelf of a high cupboard. Talk about safe use of stools, chairs, or ladders. Have the children help you rearrange the kitchen so that foods they use most often can be stored within their easy reach.

2. Have your youngsters imagine that while they are mixing up a batch of chocolate chip cookies the batter-filled bowl falls and shatters. Have them demonstrate how they would clean up the mess. Talk about the possibility of there being glass splinters in the dough, and stress that you would rather have them throw it out than to take any chances.

3. Ask your kids what they would do if they found their favorite jam had a suspicious blue slime on it and smelled like old tennis shoes. Discuss the dangers of eating spoiled foods, and talk about why some foods should not remain outside the refrigerator for any length of time. This might also be a good time to emphasize the importance of washing hands frequently while handling foods to help prevent the spread of germs.

4. Ask your children to list foods they could easily fix for breakfast without using the stove. Be sure you don't turn up your nose at their suggestions, no matter how outrageous; the main concern is that they are nutritious.

5. Ask your children to list their favorite after-school snacks that don't require use of the stove, and check to see if you have those things on hand. If not, make a shopping list.

6. Ask your children what they think the consequences should be if they leave a mess in the kitchen. Have them suggest fitting punishments. They may come up with some novel suggestions for serious consideration.

7. Have your child demonstrate how to clean up ordinary spills, such as milk, grape juice, butter, etc. This might be a good time to discuss stains too. For carpet stains, the most commonly recommended cleanup is to flood with cool water and then blot the stain with paper towels.

8. With your children, look over the dishes in your home and identify those that are microwave-safe. Discuss silver edges and metal decorations on dishes. It's a good idea to have a supply of paper plates for microwave use, too.

9. Show your children how to open a can with a manual can opener. Talk about the danger of getting cut on the sharp lid. Show the correct opener to punch holes in the lid of a large juice can.

10. Some evening when you have lots of time and patience, help your child cook a complete meal that requires use of the stove and/or oven. The youngster can plan the meal, make a shopping list, and perhaps buy the groceries in advance.

In Conclusion

Our aim is to teach children kitchen safety, simple meal preparation, and beginning culinary competence. The goal is to make their time in the kitchen satisfying to both stomach and self-esteem. Work with your children toward these goals, and they will have many pleasant memories to share with their own children years hence.

Chapter 7

TEACHING YOUR CHILDREN
FIRST AID

Brent and his friends were riding to soccer practice when Brent jumped a curb and fell off his bike. His arm looked funny and hurt terribly. Far from home, neither he nor his friends knew what to do.

Tina was at the playground when she collided with a fence and knocked out one of her permanent front teeth. She ran home and phoned her mother at work. By the time her mother got home and they finally found the tooth, three hours had passed. The dentist who tried to reimplant the tooth didn't think it would be successful since so much time had elapsed and the tooth had not been kept moist.

Ai and her friend Ruthy were eating peanuts when Ruthy began to choke. Ai hit her on the back, but that didn't help. She didn't know what else to do, so she left Ruthy and ran to a neighbor for help.

Melody and her brother, Marty, were horsing around in their apartment when Marty slipped and fell against the patio door and his hand broke through the glass. Seeing the blood spurt from Marty's wrist, Melody ran screaming down the halls of the building trying to find someone to help her brother.

Antonio was home from school with a cold. His parents went to work after getting him settled in front of the television. They told him he could take some aspirin, but the directions on the bottles were so complicated. If his mother usually gave him five baby aspirins, did that mean he should take five adult aspirins?

These stories illustrate the importance of teaching children first aid. Since accidents, both severe and minor, can occur when parents or other adults are not conveniently available, children must know what to do and how to get help. Safety experts estimate that one-third of all the youngsters home alone will someday have to face an emergency situation; often the emergency is one requiring first aid.

After you teach your children the information in this chapter, it is also a very good idea to enroll them in a children's first aid class to reinforce the skills. Call your local Red Cross, fire station, YMCA, boys or girls club, or community center to find out about first aid courses especially for children. If none are scheduled, perhaps you and other parents can ask for one to be given.

First Aid for Minor Injuries

Although minor scratches, scrapes, and cuts are not serious, proper treatment promotes healing, lessens the danger of infection, and keeps the injury from getting worse. Children also feel more confident when they know the proper things to do. Make sure your children understand these general rules for treating minor injuries.

1. Wash hands with soap and warm water before touching the wound.
2. Do not bandage a wound until it has been thoroughly cleaned out with soap and warm water.
3. Never lick or suck a wound.
4. Try to keep dirt out of a wound.
5. If necessary, apply ice to ease pain and to reduce any swelling.
6. If a bandage gets wet or dirty, change it.
7. Report even minor injuries to parents so that they can watch for signs of infection.

A number of minor injuries are discussed below in alphabetical order, together with first aid steps your children should be familiar with.

Animal Bites

Animal bites must be treated immediately and reported to the child's doctor. You should also contact the animal's owner or, if the owner cannot be found, your local animal control agency or police department, as the animal may have to be quarantined to rule out the possibility of rabies. Your child should follow these steps if bitten.

1. Wash the bite *thoroughly* with soap and warm water for at least two minutes, then cover the bite with a bandage.

2. Notify parents or other responsible adult as soon as possible, and describe the incident, where it occurred, and what the animal looked like.

Make sure you warn your children *never* to handle a wild animal, either dead or alive. A live animal that has rabies may bite, and a dead animal that was rabid can also infect a child, passing on the disease through any tiny cut, hangnail, or nick on the child's hands. Although the newer rabies shots are far less painful than the old series, no one wants to undergo them needlessly. To make your point, tell your child the following true story.

Some school children found a dead bat on the playground, picked it up, and brought it to their teacher. Unfortunately, the teacher used the dead bat to provide an interesting "hands-on" biology lesson for the class. As an afterthought the teacher took the animal to the authorities, who had it tested for rabies. The test was positive. Twenty-two people had handled the rabid bat and were exposed to rabies, and all of them had to have rabies shots to protect them from this dreaded disease.

Baby Teeth

It's natural and normal for baby teeth to come out when the permanent ones are ready to replace them, but if there's a great deal of bleeding, it can be frightening for the child. Here's what your child should do if bleeding from a baby tooth does not stop: Fold a gauze square and put it over the place where the tooth was. Bite down firmly for five minutes or until the bleeding stops. And don't forget to save the baby tooth for the Tooth Fairy! (If a permanent tooth comes out, see page 82.)

Black Eyes

Injuries that result from a hard blow to the eye should be seen by a doctor to make sure there isn't internal bleeding in the eye. Here's what children should be taught to do for immediate treatment.

1. Make a cold compress by folding a wet washcloth around pieces of ice. An unopened bag of frozen peas or corn can also be used as a cold compress. Place the compress on the eye to reduce pain and swelling.

2. If the blow was severe, notify parents or other responsible adult. Then lie down with both eyes closed and the cold compress on the injured eye.

Blisters

Teach your children these steps to treat a blister.

1. If the blister hasn't broken and won't be further irritated, cover it with a bandage or gauze pad held in place by adhesive tape. The "water" in the blister will be reabsorbed as it heals.

2. If the blister breaks, exposing raw skin, wash it carefully with soap and warm water, and cover it with a bandage or gauze pad.

3. If it looks as if the blister will be accidentally broken by repeated rubbing, carefully open the blister using this method. Wash the area with soap and warm water, and clean a needle by putting it in rubbing alcohol. Then puncture the edge of the blister with the needle, and gently press the blister to force the fluid out. Last, cover the area with a bandage or gauze pad.

Bruises

Although there is not much that can be done to treat a bruise, tell your children to apply ice or a cold compress to relieve the pain and reduce the swelling.

Burns

See page 97 to determine the severity of the burn and the correct treatment.

Cuts

First aid for severe cuts that bleed heavily is covered on page 93. Here's what your children should do for a minor cut.

1. Wash the cut, no matter how small, with soap and water.

2. If the cut continues bleeding, apply direct pressure by firmly pressing down on the wound to stop the bleeding. Minor bleeding from a cut is beneficial because it helps to wash out the germs. When the bleeding has stopped, apply a Band-Aid.

3. If the cut is deep or the edges gape and won't stay together, notify parents or other responsible adult at once. It may be necessary to have the cut stitched or sutured. Some parents prefer to have facial cuts stitched by a plastic surgeon for better cosmetic results.

Frostbite

Teach your children that frostbite occurs when a part of the body (usually the nose, fingers, or toes) starts to freeze. Before the area actually becomes frostbitten, the skin may turn slightly red in color, but as frostbite develops the skin color changes to white or grayish-white. Often there is no pain, but the part feels cold and numb. Here's what your children should do for frostbite.

1. Bring the victim indoors where it is warm.

2. Place the affected part (fingers, toes) in warm, not hot, water until the skin is flushed or reddish in color. Or place warm wet or dry cloths over the frostbitten area (ears, nose). *Don't* rub the frostbitten area. *Don't* apply ice, snow, gasoline, or anything else to the area.

3. If blisters form, cover them with a soft sterile bandage, taking care not to break them.

4. Contact parents or other responsible adult as soon as possible, as the victim may need medical attention.

Headaches

Most childhood headaches are not serious; they usually result from hunger, stress, fever, lack of sleep, or eye strain. Here's how your children should deal with a headache.

1. Don't take aspirin or other medication without first checking with your parents. The best cure is to lie down and relax in a dark room and place a cool wet cloth on the forehead.

2. Contact parents if you have a feverish headache, since these may be caused by flu, a cold, or other illness.

3. Contact parents or other responsible adult immediately if a headache comes on suddenly after a head injury or is accompanied by nausea, vomiting, blurred vision, or dizziness. These can be symptoms of a severe head injury and should be attended to at once.

Heat Exhaustion

Children can become overheated on hot days if they are very active. Here's how to deal with heat exhaustion.

1. Recognize the symptoms: pale, clammy skin; excessive sweating; and extreme weakness or fatigue.

2. Take the victim to a cool, shady, well-ventilated area; remove the victim's outer clothing, shoes, and socks; and cool the victim with fans or wet cloths.

3. Give the victim sips of cool water or other cool drinks and allow him or her to rest.

Insect Stings

To treat severe allergic reactions to insect bites, see page 103. Insect stings are a common occurrence when children play outdoors, so it's important that they know how to treat them. These are the things they should know.

1. If the stinger is still in the skin, remove it by scraping with a dull knife or pull it out gently with tweezers. Try not to squeeze the stinger, as this will release the venom.

2. When the stinger is out, make a paste out of meat tenderizer or baking soda and water, and put it on the bite. This will reduce the pain and swelling. If there are no makings for a paste, apply ice.

Knocked-Out Teeth

When a permanent tooth has been knocked out, quick treatment and proper care of the tooth are critical. Dentists are often able to reimplant the tooth if it is handled properly. Teach your children these important steps.

1. Find the tooth. If there's water handy, the tooth should be rinsed off, but not scrubbed. If water is not available and the tooth is dirty, rinse the tooth off in the mouth or spit on it to clean it.

2. Next, put the tooth back in the gum where it came from. If this is not possible, put it under the tongue to keep it moist, or wrap it in a clean, moist cloth. If water is handy, put the tooth in a glass of water to which a teaspoon of salt has been added.

3. Phone the dentist as soon as possible and arrange to go there immediately. Contact parents or other responsible adult, or if no other ride is available, call a taxi or ask the dentist to arrange transportation.

Although this is not a life-threatening emergency, proper care of the tooth and immediate care by the dentist are vital. If the tooth is whole, root and all, and the child is seen by the dentist within a half hour after the accident, there is often a good chance the tooth can be successfully reimplanted.

Nosebleeds

Nosebleeds can be very upsetting to youngsters because they come on without warning, are messy, and seem to involve a great deal of blood. Teach your children to follow these steps when dealing with a nosebleed.

1. Sit straight up and pinch both nostrils together for at least five minutes. Don't let go to see if the bleeding has stopped. If the bleeding continues after five minutes, do it again for another five minutes.

2. Don't blow your nose for a while, as that will disturb the blood clot and may start the bleeding again.

3. If the bleeding still doesn't stop (this can sometimes happen after a severe blow to the nose or face), contact parents or other responsible adult, as it may be necessary to go to the doctor.

Poisonous Plants

If poisonous plants, such as poison oak, poison ivy, or poison sumac, grow in your area, be sure that your children can recognize them easily and know to keep well away. If they do come in contact with these plants, teach them to follow these steps.

1. Go directly home, remove all clothing and set it aside, wash the affected area carefully and thoroughly with soap and water, and then swab the area with rubbing alcohol applied with a cotton ball or folded tissue.

2. If blisters form, *don't* scratch or touch them, since this may spread the irritation to other areas of the body. Instead, apply calamine lotion to relieve the itch or soak in a cool bath that contains a cup of baking soda.

You should wash the clothing that the child was wearing separately, so that the poisonous plant oils don't get on other clothing. Also, it's a good idea to buy an over-the-counter hydrocortisone ointment and teach your children to spread a thin layer over the affected area. If the area of irritation is large or extremely bothersome, take the child to the doctor.

Puncture Wounds

A puncture wound results when a sharp object such as a nail, pencil, or knife pierces the skin and tissue underneath. Usually there is little bleeding from puncture wounds. This increases the chances for infection, since germs aren't washed out by the bleeding. Teach your children these steps for treating a puncture wound.

1. If the object that caused the injury is still in the wound, *gently* try to pull it out, unless it is deeply embedded or removal is very painful.

2. Wash the wound thoroughly with soap and warm water and try to make it bleed by gently pressing on or around it. Cover the wound with a bandage or gauze pad held in place with adhesive tape.

3. If a pencil made the puncture wound, try to wash the lead out or it will leave a black mark when it has healed.

Since there is a danger of tetanus with puncture wounds, parents should check with a doctor to see if the youngster needs a shot, which can be given within forty-eight hours of the injury.

Scrapes

Scrapes (sometimes called abrasions), skinned knees, and skinned elbows are frequent childhood injuries. Since knowing how to treat them can help prevent infection, promote healing, and lessen scarring, teach your children to treat these injuries in the following way.

1. Clean the scrape by washing the dirt and gravel out gently with soap and warm water. Any dirt left in the wound may cause infection and will discolor the skin after the wound has healed.

2. If the dirt won't wash out, soak in a warm bath; this will often soak out the dirt painlessly or soften the skin so that the wound can be gently cleaned. A bath is also a good idea if the scrape wasn't cleaned and taken care of immediately after it happened. If you do not allow your youngsters to take a bath when they are alone, they could try soaking the scraped area in the sink or bowl of warm water.

3. Cover the wound with a bandage or gauze pad held in place with adhesive tape. If it's a small scrape, it can be left uncovered.

Scratches

Most scratches are minor and just need a good washing with soap and water and maybe a bandage. If an animal scratched the child badly, check with a doctor to see if the youngster needs a tetanus shot. If you notice that a scratch looks infected or becomes worse, make arrangements for your child to see a doctor.

Slivers or Splinters

Children may be able to remove a sliver by themselves if it's not too large or deeply embedded. If they want to try, here's what they should do.

1. First wash the hands, and then wash the area around the sliver to soften the skin and make removal easier. Clean a tweezers and a sharp needle by carefully washing them in soap and warm water, then dipping them in rubbing alcohol.

2. If the sliver is sticking out of the skin, gently pull it out with the tweezers. If the sliver is right below the skin and not deeply embedded, try to loosen the skin around it with the needle and carefully pull it out with the tweezers. If the sliver is deeply embedded, wait until parents come home to see whether they can remove it.

3. After removing the sliver, gently squeeze the skin so that the wound bleeds and germs are washed out. Then wash the area again with soap and water and cover it with a bandage.

If a sliver is deeply embedded, it may be necessary to have a doctor remove it.

Something in the Eye

Here's what youngsters should do if they get something in their eye.

1. Do not rub the eye since doing so may embed the particle and make the problem worse.

2. If it's a small particle of dirt or dust or an eyelash, gently pull the top eyelid out and hold it down over the bottom one. This will make the eye water, and the tears may wash out the particle. If that doesn't work, try putting the face under the faucet while holding the eye open so that cool, gently running water will flow across the eyeball.

3. If a particle is actually embedded in the eye, do not try to remove it, but cover the eye and contact parents or a responsible adult, who can take the youngster to the doctor immediately.

Sprains

Teach your children the following steps if they suspect they have sprained a limb.

1. Apply ice or cold compress as soon as possible to ease pain and reduce swelling. To make a compress, wrap ice in a wet cloth; an unopened bag of frozen vegetables such as corn or peas can also be used as an ice bag.

2. Elevate the sprained limb by putting it up on pillows, or lie on the floor with the limb up on the couch.

3. Wrap an elastic (Ace-type) bandage around the sprain to give it support and ease the discomfort.

4. Notify parents as soon as possible, since sprains should be seen by a doctor to rule out the possibility of broken bones.

Stomachaches

Most childhood stomachaches are minor, but severe stomachaches may indicate a serious problem. Teach your child to distinguish between mild and severe stomachaches and act accordingly.

1. If pain is severe, do not eat, drink, or take any medication. Contact parents, as it may be necessary to see a doctor to rule out any serious conditions.

2. If stomachache is minor it may be caused by indigestion and relieved by a bowel movement or resting quietly for a while.

3. If stomach is queasy, it may be calmed by drinking a glass of milk, a carbonated beverage, or eating a soda cracker. "Butterflies" in the stomach, caused by stress or tension, are best relieved by talking things over with an understanding friend, adult, or parent.

Superglue Accidents

Superglue accidents are more and more common these days, so your youngsters should know what to do if they get superglue on themselves. Teach them the following steps.

1. If superglue gets on the skin, put a light coat of vegetable oil over the glue and rub gently. This will usually remove the glue.

2. If the fingers, or other skin, are stuck together, do not try to pull them apart. First soak the skin in warm water or rub with vegetable oil. If that does not work, contact parents. A doctor will have to separate the bonded skin.

3. If superglue gets in the eyes, call the emergency medical number for immediate aid.

Vomiting

Since vomiting is common with flu and childhood illnesses and can be very upsetting, it's important to teach your children how to deal with nausea and vomiting.

1. Contact parents to report that you are ill, then lie down and stay quiet. It's a good idea to have a bucket or small plastic wastebasket nearby in case you are not able to get to the bathroom in time. After vomiting, rinse the mouth with water. Wiping the face with a cool, wet washcloth is also comforting.

2. Do not eat or drink anything. If you are thirsty, suck on an ice cube or ice chips.

Wind Knocked Out

When children fall on their chest or back, or are hit in the chest, they may get the wind knocked out of them. This can be frightening since the child feels unable to breathe. There's no special treatment, but a little advance knowledge of what is happening can lessen the fear. Tell your children that a hard blow to the chest may knock the extra air out of their lungs, but they will start breathing again in a few seconds. There's no treatment necessary unless the blow that knocked the wind out also produced an injury. If that's the case, they should phone you or, if the injury is severe, call the number for emergency medical aid.

Childhood Illness

Although dealing with illness may not be considered first aid, youngsters should know how to cope with being sick, since all kids seem to get their share of colds and flu no matter how careful parents are about family health.

Some parents always stay home when their youngsters are ill. They feel that being sick is stressful for a child and want to be there to care for the youngster and administer needed medicine. Other parents feel it's unnecessary to stay home every time their youngster has a minor illness such as a simple cold. Still other parents are simply unable to take time from work. As a general rule of thumb, if your child has the following symptoms, the youngster should not be left alone.

- Temperature above 101 degrees
- Vomiting or diarrhea
- Pain

As a parent you can tell the difference between real pain and the fussiness and discomfort that goes along with minor illness.

If neither parent is able to stay home or alter work schedules, it may be possible for a relative, baby-sitter, or trusted neighbor to watch the youngster. If those options are not possible, perhaps a neighbor would be willing to check on the child and bring over a meal. Some day-care facilities have special rooms for children who are ill.

If you leave a child at home when she is ill, make sure she has things to keep her occupied such as games, hobby activities, books, or television. Also either leave a lunch for her or tell her what she can fix. Be sure to phone home often to see how she's doing and to reassure her.

Sick children who take care of themselves at home alone need to know how to take their temperatures. Show them how to use your thermometer and read the temperature. Teach them not to take their temperature for at least a half hour after a bath or a hot or cold drink, as this can affect the reading. Also tell them that if the thermometer breaks, they must not play with or touch the poisonous mercury or fluid inside.

Since dosages on medicine bottles may be confusing, it's important to make sure children understand exactly how much medicine to take. While the directions for adult aspirin may call for one tablet, those on children's aspirin may call for five tablets. Children may also have difficulty figuring out how often they should take a medicine. To avoid these problems, write out the instructions or give verbal instructions to your child over the phone as he or she takes the medicine.

If your children take a liquid medicine, make sure they know exactly which spoon is a "teaspoon" and which is a "tablespoon." Some kitchens contain as many as four different-sized spoons. To be on the safe side, buy a Medispoon—a spoonlike liquid medicine dispenser. It is easier to use than a spoon, and since it holds 2 teaspoons, an accidental overdose is less likely. It is still best if children phone parents before taking any medicine to make sure they are taking the correct medication and the correct dose.

Instead of staying home with a sick youngster or leaving him home alone, some parents send a child to school when he has a minor cold. They reason that a child feels just as terrible with a cold whether he is at home or at school, recovers just as quickly in either place, and won't miss as much work if he's at school. Of course, a child with a cold is spreading his germs to classmates and must endure a day at school when he's not feeling well. It is always better not to send an ailing child to school.

If a child becomes ill at school, it may not be possible to bring him home and take care of him. Before a situation like this ever happens, it's a good idea to line up a neighbor who is willing to do this. Sometimes school personnel will drive a child home with a parent's permission if no other arrangements can be made. If there's no one to stay with the youngster until you get home, make sure the child can get into the house and knows to lie down and rest quietly. Ask the youngster to phone you, your spouse, or a coworker to let you know he's home and settled.

Sometimes sick children can stay in the school infirmary or nurse's room until school ends, but most schools prefer to have them taken home since the schools usually do not have full-time nurses on staff and they don't want the child spreading germs.

Children with Chronic Medical Conditions

If children with chronic health conditions such as asthma or epilepsy are alone at home, make sure they know how to deal with these problems by themselves, if that's possible. If the youngster cannot manage the condition herself and you still choose to let her stay alone, you should check into some of these options.

1. Consider paying a nearby neighbor to check on your child regularly. If there is a problem, make sure the neighbor knows *exactly* what to do. Post complete instructions for dealing with the child's medical condition, the emergency medical number, the doctor's phone number, your number at work, what medicine, if any, to administer, and so on. Post these instructions in a conspicuous place such as on the refrigerator door. This information may also be useful to emergency personnel who might be summoned.

2. Check into some of the newer electronic beepers that can be worn by people with severe medical conditions. The device summons medical personnel to your address when the wearer has an emergency. Most devices are tied into the phone system and programmed to ring into a main switchboard or emergency medical phone number in your area. Some can be programmed to summon a nearby relative or neighbor. The device is usually activated when the wearer pushes an alarm button, but some even activate with pressure, for instance, when the wearer falls down.

Your local hospital or physician can give you more information about these units.

Life-Threatening Emergencies

Youngsters are less likely to face a serious emergency, but it's still advisable for them to be prepared to handle one, since correct action could save a life. When you teach your children these skills, try to tailor the information to their age and ability, but first make sure they understand these rules.

Do not panic — Tell your children they must not panic during an emergency, since panic upsets both them and the victim and makes the situation worse. Teach them to take a few deep breaths to calm themselves.

Do not move the victim — Teach your children to try to avoid moving a severely injured or unconscious victim; if the victim's spine or neck has been injured, further movement will worsen the injury. However, if leaving the victim where he is will result in more serious injury or death, he must be *gently* moved. For instance, an injured person would have to be gently dragged out of a burning house whether or not his neck was injured or he would certainly die in the fire.

Get adult help — During a serious or life-threatening emergency, youngsters must get adult help, so teach them not to be embarrassed or hesitant to ask for assistance and, if necessary, to *insist* on it. Frequently adults are slow to take children seriously, so youngsters must be assertive. Reassure them that if what they thought was a severe emergency turns out to be only a minor problem, they are still better off playing it safe than taking a chance. Tell your child that if someone is using the phone or on a party line when he needs to phone for emergency help, the youngster should state that it is against the law for anyone to refuse to yield the phone when someone is trying to report an emergency.

Memorize emergency phone numbers in your area – If they cannot remember a phone number they can dial the operator, but that extra call takes valuable time. However, if children happen to be in another city or unfamiliar area when an emergency arises, have them dial the operator rather than waste time looking up emergency numbers. Make sure your children know they should phone emergency services such as ambulance or police immediately and not waste time calling or going to a neighbor, who may not be home.

Speak slowly and clearly – When reporting an emergency, they should state their name, address, and cross street or location of the emergency; the nature of the problem; and the kind of help that is needed. They should not hesitate to repeat this information if the person on the other end of the phone doesn't get all of the message the first time. They also should not hang up until they are told to do so, because often emergency personnel will keep them on the line to give them instructions while help is being sent.

Fill out emergency forms – On page 207 there is an emergency phone number form to fill out, make copies of, and post by all the phones in your house so that this information is handy during an emergency. You might also ask if you can do this for your neighbors' phones. Do not count on being able to remember vital information in a crisis. Make sure it is there by the phone, immediately available to your children or yourself when it is needed.

Serious and life-threatening emergencies are listed in alphabetical order for ease in reference.

Bleeding

Heavy bleeding from a major blood vessel can quickly lead to death unless it is stopped. If the victim is spurting blood or losing one-fourth to one-half a cup of blood or more, this should be considered heavy bleeding. In this emergency the child should *first* stop the bleeding by applying direct pressure, *then* phone for emergency help. These are the steps to teach your child.

1. To stop heavy bleeding, put a sterile pad or handy clean cloth over the cut; if nothing else is available, use your bare hand. Press down on the wound, keeping fingers flat so they won't dig into the cut. If the wound is on an arm or leg, elevate the limb higher than the victim's heart; this will slow the bleeding. But do not elevate the limb if it appears to be broken or if elevating hurts the victim.

2. If blood soaks through the first pad or cloth, do not remove it. Just add more layers and continue applying direct pressure. It may take five minutes or more of direct pressure before the blood begins to clot and the heavy bleeding stops.

3. After the heavy bleeding stops, phone for emergency medical help. The wound can be bandaged firmly, but not tightly, and the victim should be observed for signs of shock. (See page 105 for information on shock.)

If you think your child knows about tourniquets (a bandage around an arm or leg that is tightened by twisting with a stick) and might attempt to use one, make it clear that tourniquets are very rarely used and should not be attempted by a child. Direct pressure will almost always do the job. Teach your child that if he is alone and bleeding badly, he should apply direct pressure on the wound while he is phoning for an ambulance.

Breathing Emergencies

If a person has stopped breathing (because of electrical shock, drowning, etc.), it is vital to get air moving in and out of her lungs at once; without air, she has only minutes (often less than 5) before permanent brain damage and death may occur. Most youngsters 9 and older can master mouth-to-mouth breathing. Teach your children these steps. If your child finds someone unconscious, the youngster should immediately check to see whether the person is breathing by watching to see if his chest rises and falls. Another way is for the child to put his ear near the victim's mouth to listen for the entry or exit of air. If the victim is not breathing, the child should follow these steps.

1. Phone the emergency medical number to summon an ambulance before beginning mouth-to-mouth breathing; once mouth-to-mouth breathing is started, it must not be stopped until relief comes or the victim breathes on his own. If another person is present, that person should make the emergency call.

2. ·Gently turn the victim on his back, open his mouth, and sweep your fingers quickly around in the victim's mouth to clear it of any foreign matter.

3. Tip the victim's head back, and open his jaws by pulling up on the lower jaw so it juts outward (Figure 1).

4. Pinch the victim's nose closed and then place your mouth over the victim's mouth, making an airtight seal. If the victim is an infant, baby, or young child, put your mouth over both the child's mouth and nose, making an airtight seal (Figure 2).

5. Blow two full breaths into the victim's mouth.

6. With the victim's nose still pinched shut and his head back, breathe into the victim's mouth every five seconds for an adult, every four seconds for a child, and every three seconds for an infant. Remove your mouth from the victim's mouth between breaths.

7. After a few breaths, put your ear close to the victim's mouth to listen for air leaving the victim's lungs. See if his chest rises when air enters and falls when air is exhaled.

8. If the entry or return of air seems blocked or if the victim's chest does not rise, an obstruction may be blocking his air-

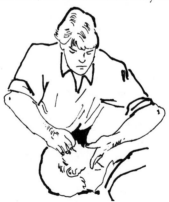

Figure 1

Figure 2

way. If this is the case, clear the airway before continuing mouth-to-mouth breathing (see "Choking," page 98). After the airway is cleared, again give breaths every five seconds for adults, four seconds for children, and every three seconds for infants.

9. Continue mouth-to-mouth breathing until the victim can breathe on his own or until medical personnel arrive to take over. It is sometimes necessary to continue mouth-to-mouth breathing as long as thirty minutes before the victim is able to breathe on his own.

When teaching mouth-to-mouth breathing to your youngsters, it's a good idea to warn them that often the victim vomits during or before this procedure. Although this may seem "gross," the rescuer must not stop. The rescuer should turn the victim's head to the side, clear out the mouth, reposition the head, and continue mouth-to-mouth breathing. Teach your children that when a life is at stake, it is possible to endure something "gross."

Broken Bones

Most broken bones are not life-threatening, but further damage may be done if they are not treated properly. Although some broken bones do not cause much pain, your child should suspect a broken bone if the injured limb does not look normal and hurts a great deal. Also, you can't always tell if a bone is broken by looking at it. Only a doctor can tell for sure by taking an x-ray. If the child suspects a broken bone, she should follow these steps, and if it turns out that the injured part is not broken, so much the better.

1. The victim should not be moved unless she is in danger. If she must be moved, take care to support the injured part and avoid bumping or jostling it.

2. The victim should be kept lying down and calm. Do not attempt to splint the broken bone unless you have been specially trained to do this.

3. Place an ice pack or cold compress on the injured part to reduce the pain and swelling, but avoid freezing the area.

4. Call for medical help or get an adult to drive the victim to a hospital or doctor's office. During the trip the injured part should be supported so that it doesn't move around.

COMPOUND FRACTURES

Teach your children that a compound fracture is a sharp broken bone that has punctured the skin. It is a very serious kind of break. If there is heavy bleeding, the child may need to use direct pressure to stop the flow, but since the bone is broken, care should be taken to not press too hard or move the bone. The child should call for emergency medical help immediately.

Burns

Since burns must be treated according to their severity, it is important to teach your children how to determine this.

First-degree burns – These are the least severe burns. The skin is red and painful, but blisters are not present and the skin is not broken. A sunburn or burns caused by brief contact with hot objects are usually first-degree burns. They can usually be treated at home, but if they are on the face or near the eyes, they should be seen by a doctor.

Second-degree burns – Second-degree burns are burns that cause injury to the layers of the skin beneath the surface. They cause swelling, pain, and blisters. A deep sunburn or burns from hot liquids are examples of this type of burn. If a second-degree burn is large, if it is on the face, around the nose or mouth, or on the hands, or if the victim has inhaled flames or hot vapors, medical help is needed.

Third-degree burns – These burns destroy all layers of the skin so that the burned area is either white or charred. There may be little pain because nerve endings have been destroyed. Burns that result from a fire, prolonged contact with hot substances, or electricity are examples of third-degree burns. Third-degree burns are the most serious and need immediate medical attention.

These are the steps to teach your children in dealing with burns.

1. Immediately cool *all* burns by running cool water over them or applying cool water (*not ice or ice water*) with a clean towel, washcloth, etc. This reduces the heat, lessens the injury, and helps relieve the pain. *Do not* put butter, oils, toothpaste, aloe plants, or other home remedies on a burn.

2. Bandage the burn with a sterile dressing or clean cloth. If clothing is stuck to the burn, do not attempt to remove it. Just put the clean dressing over it and phone for medical help. Blisters that form should not be broken.

Chemical Burns

Strong chemicals such as acids or cleaning products can cause serious burns to the skin or eyes. These are the steps to teach your children if this happens.

SKIN

1. Carefully remove any clothing that came into contact with the chemical.

2. Wash the chemical off quickly by running cool water over the area for *at least* five minutes. Do not use soap or scrub the skin, as this will make the injury worse.

3. Call the poison control center to see if any additional steps should be taken.

EYES

1. Wash out the eyes *immediately*. Either put your head in the sink or get into the shower; hold the affected eye open with your fingers and let tepid or cool water flow over the eyeball for *at least* five minutes.

2. Call the emergency medical number for help.

3. Put a clean towel over the eyes like a blindfold and wait until emergency medical help arrives.

Choking

Your child should suspect choking if someone collapses while eating; begins coughing, gasping, wheezing, or grabbing at the throat; or turns white or blue in the face. Since choking is a common emergency, it is important that your child know what to do. Teach your children the signs of choking and the steps to follow for both conscious and unconscious victims.

FOR A CONSCIOUS PERSON

1. If the victim is coughing or can talk, no interference is necessary, since the victim may be able to cough up the object. The rescuer should watch the victim carefully, however, and stay with him if he gets up and moves around.

2. If the victim is not coughing or making any noise, his airway is probably blocked and the rescuer should proceed to the next step.

3. Stand behind the victim, who may be standing or sitting. Put your arms under the victim's arms and around the victim's waist. Place your fist with the thumb side against the victim's stomach just slightly above the victim's navel (belly button) and below the ribs. Hold your fist with your other hand and give the victim four quick, forceful, inward thrusts. Do not squeeze with your arms, but thrust inward and slightly upward with the fists. These thrusts increase the pressure in the victim's abdomen and push up the diaphragm, which in turn increases the air pressure in the lungs, thus forcing out the object blocking the airway (Figures 3 and 4).

4. If the victim is a pregnant woman or a fat person, stand behind the victim and place your arms under the victim's arms at armpit height. Then place the thumb side of the fist on the

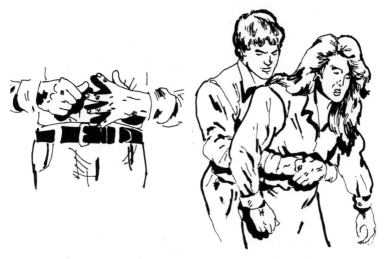

Figure 3   **Figure 4**

victim's midchest over the breastbone. Hold the fist with the other hand and give the victim four quick, inward thrusts (Figure 5).

5. Repeat the thrusts until the victim's airway is cleared or until emergency personnel arrive to take over. If the object that choked the victim moves up into his mouth or throat, reach in and gently remove it.

FOR AN UNCONSCIOUS PERSON

1. Gently turn the victim on his back and kneel at his side.

2. Place the heel of your hand on the victim's stomach, slightly above his navel and below his ribs.

3. Keeping your elbows straight, put your free hand on top of the other hand and give four quick, forceful, downward thrusts (Figure 6).

FOR CHILDREN AND INFANTS

Both the above methods can be used for children, but they should be done gently. When performing thrusts on an infant, use two fingers, not the fist, placed on the infant's stomach above

Figure 5

his navel and below his ribs. Or place the infant over your arm
or knee, and give a quick blow between his shoulder blades.

ALONE AND CHOKING

Teach your child that if he is alone and chokes on something,
he should try to give himself abdominal thrusts by pressing his
fist between his rib cage and navel and giving a quick upward
thrust. The child can also lean forward and press his abdomen
quickly and forcefully against a firm object such as a chair back,
counter, or a porch railing. If that doesn't work, he should try
to get to a neighbor's before becoming unconscious.

PREVENTION IS THE BEST MEDICINE

Choking can often be prevented. Teach your children that
no one, no matter what age, should swallow food until it has been
thoroughly chewed. Both parents and older children who baby-
sit siblings or other youngsters should follow these precautions.

Figure 6

1. Don't let babies or toddlers play with any object small enough to put in their mouths.

2. Don't let babies and toddlers eat solid foods unless they are sitting up.

3. Don't allow babies or toddlers to eat things like peanuts, hot dogs, grapes, olives with pits, hard candies, etc.

Electrical Shocks

Powerful shocks can come from electrical appliances, wires, or outlets if they are not properly handled. These shocks can give a severe jolt to, or even kill, a person. Teach your children how to handle an electrical shock.

1. If a victim has gotten a severe electrical shock and is still in contact with the power source, do *not* touch the person or the power source until the power has been turned off. This can be done by unplugging the appliance (or power source), throwing the circuit breaker, or removing the fuse in the fuse box. (Be sure to show your children the location of your circuit breaker or fuse box and how it operates.)

2. If you are unable to turn off the power, do not attempt a rescue. Call for emergency help and leave this dangerous rescue to the experts. *Do not* attempt to pull or push the victim away from the power. If you touch the victim or the power source when the power is still on, you too will receive a severe or killing shock.

3. Once the power is off, call for emergency medical aid, then check to see if the victim is breathing.

4. If the victim is not breathing, administer mouth-to-mouth breathing (page 94); keep it up until help arrives or the person breathes on her own.

5. Finally, treat the victim for shock (page 104) and burns (page 96).

Head Injuries

Most head injuries are just simple bumps and lumps of everyday living, but severe head injuries can be life-threatening and need immediate medical attention. Teach your child to observe the victim after head injury and treat accordingly.

1. If blood or clear fluid comes from a victim's nose, mouth, or ears after a fall or injury, call for immediate medical aid. Then keep the victim quiet and warm; do not move the victim until help arrives.

2. If a person is stunned or dizzy after a fall or injury, make him lie down and rest. Watch for signs of serious head injury: headache, nausea or vomiting, signs of weakness or confusion, or enlarged pupils. If any of these signs are present, summon medical aid immediately.

Heart Stoppage

When a person's heart stops, cardiopulmonary resuscitation (CPR) should be done at once. CPR is an advanced technique of mouth-to-mouth breathing combined with chest compressions. Most children over 10 are capable of learning CPR. CPR cannot effectively be learned from a book alone, since equipment for practice and a trained instructor are necessary. *It is highly recommended that your entire family take a CPR course.* Call your local American Heart Association, Red Cross, hospital, or fire department to schedule a class. Ask friends and neighbors to join you.

Insect Stings

Most stings are just a quick pain, but to people who are allergic to the venom, this can be a life-threatening situation. If a member of your family reacts severely to insect stings, you should always have an insect sting kit available and all family members should know how to use it. Tell your youngsters that if they or anyone they are with ever has trouble breathing or feels weak or nauseated after an insect sting, they need to call for medical help immediately. If the person passes out, administer mouth-to-mouth resuscitation.

Poisoning

Many products in the home can act as poisons if they are swallowed, mixed, or used improperly. Even a helpful medicine can act as a poison if too much of it is taken. Since poisoning is one of the most common life-threatening emergencies, it is vital that you teach your youngsters how to treat it.

How can a child tell if someone has been poisoned other than seeing the victim eat or swallow the poison? The victim may be unconscious, may have burns on his mouth or face from swallowing a poisonous chemical, may be acting strangely for no apparent reason, or may seem to be drugged or drunk. Also there may be a bottle or container of the poison near the victim.

Teach your children the following steps.

1. *Quickly* try to find the container that held the poison.

2. Call the nearest poison center to get help. If there is no poison center in the area, call the emergency medical number, the hospital, or a doctor.

3. Follow the directions given by the poison center or medical personnel.

4. *Do not* make the victim vomit unless the poison center or medical personnel gives those instructions, since some poisons burn the mouth and throat when swallowed and burn again when vomited back up.

5. If the victim is conscious, the rescuer should give him water if this can be done quickly. Only water, nothing else, should be given.

POISON PREVENTION

The best way to avoid poisoning is to prevent it. Teach your children to follow these rules at home or, if they baby-sit, in other people's homes.

1. Keep medicines, cleaning products, insecticides, and other harmful products out of reach of young children. Follow directions carefully, and never experiment with or improperly use such products.

2. Always keep poisonous products in their original containers, and be sure they are properly marked.

3. When giving medicine, read directions and dosages very carefully. Never pretend medicine is candy.

4. Make sure youngsters in your care do not eat outdoor plants, berries, wild mushrooms, or any plant part that is not known to be edible.

5. Never mix laundry bleach and household ammonia together because these common cleaners produce toxic fumes.

Shock

Make sure your children understand the difference between electrical shock and medical shock. Medical shock can result when a person has been poisoned, seriously burned, or injured; suffered heavy loss of blood; or received a severe electrical shock. Medical shock is life-threatening. It slows down and weakens the body's functions and can keep the heart, lungs, and other organs from working properly, so even if the injuries do not lead directly to death, the victim can die from shock.

Teach your children to recognize these signs of shock: The victim's face may be pale and the eyes dull and empty-looking. The breathing is shallow and rapid, and the skin is cold and clammy. The victim may tremble or shake. He may vomit or feel nauseated. He may act confused and may not know where he is or what is happening. Tell your youngsters to follow these steps for shock.

1. Call for medical help if this hasn't already been done.

2. Make the victim lie down, cover him to keep him warm, and make sure he remains quiet. He should be comforted and reassured to keep his mind off his injuries.

3. If there is no possibility that the victim has injured his back or spine, raise his feet so they are above his heart, unless doing so hurts him.

Snakebite or Spider Bites

If poisonous snakes or spiders are a problem in your area, make very sure your children know how to recognize them. Also teach them to stay away from areas where poisonous snakes or spiders may live or hide. If they are bitten, they should call for emergency medical help immediately.

Activities for Practice

Prepare a Home First Aid Kit

Here's what a well-stocked first aid kit contains:

_____ Bandages in various sizes

_____ Sterile, nonstick gauze pads

_____ Adhesive tape

_____ Triangular bandage (for arm sling or bandage)

_____ Elastic bandage (for wrapping sprains)

_____ Thermometer

_____ Children's and adult aspirin or acetaminophen (to be used only under adult direction)

_____ Rubbing alcohol (for sterilizing items)

_____ Scissors, tweezers, and needle (for removing slivers)

_____ Ice pack or Instant Ice (to control swelling)

_____ Calamine lotion and hydrocortisone ointment (to relieve itching)

_____ Cold tablets and other medicines used by family (to be used only under adult direction)

_____ Syrup of Ipecac (to induce vomiting, only if directed by poison center, doctor, or medical personnel)

_____ Insect sting kit (if a family member is known to be allergic to insect stings)

_____ Snake bite kit (if poisonous snakes are a problem in your area and medical help is not readily available)

Children responsible enough to be left home alone should have access to a family first aid kit. Assemble the items on the list. Find a plastic box, shoe box, or the like to hold them. As you put in each item, go over its use with your child. Keep the first aid kit where it is easily accessible to older children, yet out of reach of young children. Emphasize that items in the first aid kit are not for play: Bandages used to wrap a wounded teddy bear won't be there in a real emergency. Be sure to replace items as soon as they are used, and replace any medicines that are old or out of date.

Practice Reporting an Emergency

Have your children make simulated emergency phone calls to report the following medical emergencies. The parent should take the part of the emergency dispatcher, aid unit, or ambulance dispatcher who answers the call. Make sure the child speaks clearly and slowly and gives all the information needed (see page 92).

Have your child call an ambulance for a friend who may have broken her leg falling from a tree.

Have the youngster call the poison center or emergency number to report that his sister just ate a bright red mushroom that was growing in the yard.

Have the youngster report that his friend just stepped on a downed power line and received a severe shock.

Ask your child to report that a neighbor was just stung by a bee and is now gasping for breath.

Practice Administering First Aid Treatment

Ask your children to show and tell how they would deal with the following first aid situations. If they are not sure or make mistakes, review that particular section of this chapter to correct the mistakes and reinforce the learning.

BREATHING EMERGENCIES

Your youngster comes home to find his older brother unconscious on the kitchen floor. Ask him what he will do.

Some kids are playing on a rope swing that gets caught around a child's neck and chokes him. When the rope is untangled the youngster is not breathing. Ask your child what she will do.

Your child is home alone and begins to choke on a hot dog. Ask your youngster what he will do.

Your child's friend chokes on a peanut and can't cough or make any noise. Ask your child what she will do.

Your child's aunt, who is pregnant, chokes on a piece of food and cannot breathe. Ask your child what he should do.

Your child's sister chokes on some meat and falls to the floor unconscious. Ask your child what she will do.

SEVERE BLEEDING

Your child's brother breaks the glass door and severely cuts his leg. Ask your child what he should do.

Your child's friend severely cuts her foot on some glass at the beach. Neither child has any extra clothing to press against the wound. Ask your child what she will do.

While home alone, your child drops a knife on his foot, cutting himself badly. What will he do?

BURNS

Your child's younger brother has burned his hand on smoldering coals from last night's bonfire. The burned area is charred. Ask your child how severe this burn is and how it should be treated.

Your child's sister is cooking dinner when grease splatters and burns her arm. The burn is red and blistered. Ask your child how severe this burn is and how it should be treated.

While getting toast out of the toaster, your child burns his hand. The burn is red and hurts a lot. Ask your child if this is serious and how she will treat it.

While your child is loading the dishwasher, he drops dishwasher detergent on the counter and particles fly up and get in his eye. Ask him what he will do.

HEAD INJURIES

Your child's friend has fallen from the swing and hit his head. He feels dizzy and begins to vomit. Ask your child what she will do.

A child hit by a car is unconscious. There is clear fluid draining from his nose and ears. Ask your child if this is serious and what should be done.

POISONING

Your child's baby cousin comes out of the bathroom chewing on something and holding a half-empty bottle of baby aspirin. The bottle was full earlier. Ask your child what she should do.

Your child's cousin swallowed some gasoline and his mother wants to make him vomit. Ask your child if that is correct.

Your child suddenly realizes that instead of taking 2 teaspoons of a cold medicine, she got the spoons mixed up and took 2 tablespoons. Ask your youngster what she will do.

SHOCK

A friend of your child cut himself badly chopping wood. The bleeding has stopped, but he is looking pale and acting confused. Ask your child what is happening and how he will deal with it.

A friend of your child has taken a bad fall from a tree and may have broken her leg. It will take fifteen minutes for the ambulance to arrive. Your child notices her friend's face is pale, her breathing is fast, and she is acting confused. Ask your child what she will do.

ELECTRICAL SHOCK

Some electrical wires are down after a severe windstorm. The neighbor steps on a wire and gets a severe shock. He is still in contact with the live wire. Ask your child what should be done.

A toddler that your child is watching pokes a paper clip into an electrical outlet, gets a severe shock, and is unconscious. The lights in that part of the house go out. Ask your child what he will do.

BROKEN BONES

Your child and his friend are riding bikes when the friend takes a bad fall. His leg looks "funny" and he's in a great deal of pain. Ask your youngster what he will do.

After a fall, your child's arm looks misshapen, but it doesn't hurt very much. Ask her what she will do.

MINOR INJURIES

While playing soccer, your child falls and skins his knee. Nothing is done about the injury until the child is home an hour later. Ask your youngster how he will treat this skinned knee now.

Your child steps on a nail in the empty lot nearby. Ask your child how she will treat this puncture wound.

Your sons are fighting over a pencil. The youngest gets poked in the arm with the lead. The piece of lead is still stuck in the wound. Ask your child how he will treat this wound.

Your youngster has gotten a sliver from the broom handle. It isn't deep, and one end is outside the skin. Ask your child what she will do.

Your child is hit in the nose and it starts to bleed. He pinches it for five minutes, then five more minutes, but it just won't stop. Ask the youngster what he will do.

While in the woods, your child notices that she has been playing in a patch of poison oak. Ask your child what she will do.

A bee stings your child. He knows he is not allergic because he has been stung before. Ask your child what he will do.

Your child gets into a fight on the way home and gets hit in the eye. Ask her how she will treat this "black eye."

Your child falls and knocks out one of his permanent teeth. Ask him what he will do.

Your child gets a tiny particle of dirt in her eye. How will she get it out?

DEMONSTRATIONS

Gather some bottles and boxes of medicine. Ask your son to read the directions and tell you the correct dosage for his age and how often he should repeat it.

Put out four sizes of spoons and ask your daughter to point out which is a teaspoon and which is a tablespoon.

Ask your child to put a variety of bandages on a variety of pretend wounds.

In Conclusion

We know there is nothing we can do to protect our children from bumps, bruises, and scrapes, the common injuries of childhood. But we must also face the fact that more severe and even life-threatening injuries may befall our youngsters when we are not with them. To help children keep themselves safe and sound, we must teach them all we can about dealing with injuries and emergencies.

Chapter 8

KEEPING CHILDREN SAFE
FROM SEXUAL ASSAULT

The sexual abuse of children is an age-old problem. We know from biblical references, Greek mythology, and other ancient writings that it has been around for centuries; in fact, the sexual abuse of children is as old as evil itself.

In spite of this, until recently child molestation wasn't a proper subject for polite conversation; nor was it a subject parents discussed with their children, except to warn them of "dangerous strangers." Many parents believed that if they taught their children about sexual assault, the youngsters would develop a false and perverse view of human sexuality. The truth is that the subject of sexual assault belongs more in the category of violence than sexuality. To avoid teaching youngsters about sexual assault will only make them more vulnerable: Not only will they lack knowledge of the subject, but they will not learn the skills which could help them avoid or forestall sexual abuse.

We parents do not have to sit silent and powerless while sexual abuse affects more and more helpless children. We can undo the dark wraps of secrecy and make this simply another part of the personal safety information we teach our youngsters. Information on sexual assault should be taught with the same openness that accompanies information on abduction prevention and first aid. Once children are taught how to recognize and deal with potential abuse and abusers, they are better able to keep themselves safe and sound.

"Sexual abuse" or "sexual assault" (the terms are interchangeable) is defined as any contact or interaction between a child and an adult, or between a younger child and an older child, in which the perpetrator seeks or gains sexual excitement or sexual gratification through the child. It is any sexual contact made by physical force or psychological coercion that involves the handling of a child's genitals, or penetration of the child's vagina, anus, or mouth, however slight, by a penis or other object. Actual sexual contact is not always a factor: If a child is forced to look at the genitals of an adult or an older child, or is undressed and exposed, this constitutes sexual abuse. The most common forms of sexual abuse are exhibitionism and the handling of the genitals; actual penetration is rare.

It must be recognized that sexual abuse is *not* the normal curiosity young children have about their sexual organs. It is not "playing doctor" or examining one another's genitals. Those incidents are simply *normal childhood curiosity,* and most child-care specialists recommend that parents treat such incidents as normal but try to divert the children's attention to other, more socially acceptable behavior.

Sexual Abuse: Myth versus Reality

We tend to think sexual abuse is a rare and extreme threat to our children, yet the reality is that it is common—shockingly common. In the United States, at least one in four girls and one in ten boys will be sexually assaulted in some way or other before reaching the age of 18. There are other estimates that say almost half of all children will be sexually assaulted in some way before they are 18 years old. More children between the ages of 8 and 12 are sexually assaulted than teenagers, and at least 10 percent of the children assaulted are under the age of 5.

We also tend to think that most sexual assaults on children are committed by strangers, but this is not true. Over 85 percent of the child victims are assaulted by relatives, friends of the family, or acquaintances—all people the child knows and generally trusts. Only 15 percent of child sexual abuse is perpetrated by a total stranger.

Another myth is that only girls are sexually assaulted. Incidents involving sexual assaults on girls are more frequently reported, but some experts think there may be about a 50:50 distribution of male and female child victims. Boys are more reluctant to report sexual abuse for fear it may be construed as homosexual activity; also they may think it isn't "manly" to be frightened or concerned about such incidents. Most boys naively believe that only girls can be raped, but this is not true. Rape is defined as a penis or any other object penetrating the vagina, mouth, or anus. Rather than have your sons mistakenly believe they are immune to rape, it's better to be candid about this.

Adults imagine that the abuser forces children into sexual contact, but this is rarely the case. More commonly, child victims are tricked, bribed, coerced, or threatened. They are often told this behavior is perfectly normal, that everyone does it, and are shown pornographic pictures of children to enforce this belief. Victims are often bribed by offers of money, gifts, toys, or other desired objects. Children may originally be drawn in by the excitement of sharing a special secret with an older person, or they may be coerced by threats to harm them or other family members. They may even be threatened with the withdrawal of affection if the offender is a family member or someone close to the family. They may also be told their parents will punish them if they find out they have been involved in such forbidden behavior.

We tend to view sexual assault as a one-time incident that comes out of the blue, yet it is much more likely to be a gradually developing situation that progresses over a period of years. The sexual abuse of a child is rarely an isolated, one-time incident. Since there are many forms of sexual abuse, from exhibitionism to rape, the incidents tend to progress in severity and intensity. When the problem escalates gradually from what might be construed as accidental contact to obvious sexual activity, the child finds it difficult to know when to get help because one situation is hardly different from the next, yet one incident leads to another and so on. Because of this progression, children are often hesitant to report the abuse since they fear they will be blamed for not ending the chain of events much sooner.

Abusers and their victims can come from any race, ethnic group, income level, or educational background. No class or group of people is immune to the threat of child sexual assault.

Some people tend to think both men and women sexually abuse youngsters, yet statistics show that 95 percent of all child sexual abuse incidents are perpetrated by men. Of incestuous relationships, father-daughter incest is the one most commonly reported. Mother-son, mother-daughter, or father-son involvement appears to be less common.

Since there are so many kinds of sexual assault, some people feel it's simply a part of growing up and wouldn't be as big a problem if the public didn't make so much of it. Society also falsely reasons if a child has not been killed or injured, then the crime is not serious. It was previously thought that children easily forgot sexual abuse, especially if there was no force involved.

In-depth studies of the long-term effects of sexual abuse have proven these views are romanticized myths—not cold reality. Victims of childhood sexual abuse often suffer lifelong feelings of shame, guilt, mistrust of people, and abnormal sexual feelings. They are also less likely to have successful marriages. Previously it was thought that all the stigma of a sexual abuse incident rested solely on the abuser, but studies show that most youngsters feel they are somehow responsible for the incident and this self-blame, guilt, and shame often dominate the life of the child, the teen, and the adult he or she grows up to become. Any act so damaging to a child's future life can never be considered "no big problem." Without a doubt, sexual abuse is harmful to all victims and destructive to many.

It's a myth that children often fabricate stories about sexual abuse. Children who report sexual assault are rarely lying or fantasizing; the reports are almost always true. If a child has made up a story, this usually comes to light very quickly during the process of questioning. Society errs on the side of not believing reports rather than believing untrue stories.

It's also a myth to think we can completely protect our children from sexual assault. Recently there has been a great deal of interest in setting up a system of fingerprinting adults who work with children and establishing computer linkups which will disclose any known sexual offenders. This could be helpful, even though the majority of sexual offenders do not have previous records of sexual assault.

The best prevention still lies in the education of our youngsters. If we parents can convince our children they have control

over their own bodies and can teach them to say *no* to any type
of sexual assault, we have given them the best protection we can.

Talking to Children about Sexual Assault

We try to raise our children to be polite and obedient, but unfortunately these qualities can also make them more vulnerable
to sexual abuse. We tell kids to obey adults or older children in
positions of authority, such as baby-sitters, teachers, and neighbors: "Be good, mind the baby-sitter, and do as you're told." We
tell our children not to hurt people's feelings or raise a fuss:
"Don't hurt Grandpa's feelings; he just likes to hold you." Sometimes we even belittle our children when they express feelings
of discomfort over the way they're handled: "Don't be such a
baby. Uncle George just wanted to tickle you. Be nice to him."

We must amend these teachings. Children should not be
mindless robots, trusting all people without question. We should
teach them to trust their own feelings and let them know their
own personal safety comes before being a nice child. We must
let our children know they are in charge of their own bodies and
have the right to say *no* to anyone.

Even in today's more enlightened times, it's hard to talk to
kids about sexual abuse. While public-awareness efforts over the
last five to seven years have opened up and demystified this subject to a great degree, parents still find it difficult and embarrassing to talk about sexual assault. Here are some suggestions
for making this discussion as comfortable, successful, and effective as possible.

1. Before you present this subject to your children, you may
need to be educated yourself. Many parents know little about
sexual abuse. Read over the information in this chapter, then
put it into your own words. Don't be afraid to alter the teaching,
since you know what will be the most effective for your own particular child.

2. Choose a quiet time when you and your child are relaxed
and not rushed. A discussion cut short because either parent or
child has to rush off somewhere won't be nearly as effective as
one when you both have undisturbed time together.

3. This sort of teaching is not a one-time event. It becomes an ongoing process as your child grows, matures, and needs more information. The advice you give a 10-year-old will necessarily be more complex than what you might give a 5-year-old. There will be many opportunities to bring up the subject. Newspaper articles, television reports, and real-life situations are all appropriate times to reinforce the sexual abuse prevention skills you have taught your child.

4. You may be embarrassed about certain aspects of the topic of sexual abuse. It's all right to be embarrassed, but it is not all right to avoid teaching this subject because of your embarrassment. If your child asks you personal questions that you feel uncomfortable answering, just say that you don't want to answer that particular question because it's personal. Most children will respect this.

5. End your conversation by telling your children how special and precious they are to you and how important it is for them to learn to keep themselves safe.

Most youngsters have some awareness about sexual abuse. They may have overheard talk about it from adults or other children, read about the topic, or seen something on television. They may have experienced abuse personally or been told about it happening to a close friend. When you begin talking about this subject, ask your child what he or she already knows about sexual assault. Your child may have some misconception, exaggeration, or misinformation that needs to be cleared up.

Having special names for parts of the body may lead children to think these parts are bad, secret, or not to be discussed. These feelings contribute to keeping sexual abuse a deep dark secret. It's best for parents to use correct medical names for all parts of the body, including the genitals. When our children were young we didn't hesitate to teach them the names for their eyes, mouth, nose, chin, hands, and arms, but most of us stopped at the neck and began again at the knees! If you feel too uncomfortable using the terms "penis," "vagina," and "anus," call these organs "private parts" and explain to your child that the private parts are the areas of one's body covered by a swimsuit.

Children who have grown up knowing the correct names for

body parts treat the terms in a matter-of-fact way. Children for whom the terms are new are often inclined to giggle and titter with embarrassment. Parents who just ignore the giggles and continue on will find the amusement and embarrassment soon passes.

One comfortable and easily understood way to begin teaching about sexual abuse is to use the subject of touch—different kinds of touch. Everyone is familiar with touches, and kids easily relate to this introduction.

Begin by telling your children that everyone needs to be touched. This need for touch is a common human need, no matter how young or how old we are. Then explain that there are different kinds of touches. There are touches we like, such as a hug or a pat on the back. There are touches we don't like, such as a slap, punch, or kick. There are some confusing touches, such as lengthy tickling or touches on private parts of the body.

We know we like the good touches and don't like the bad ones. It's the confusing touches we aren't too sure about. We may not always understand these confusing touches, but we usually know they do not feel right. Ask your child to give you examples of the three kinds of touches. If he or she falters, here are some suggestions.

Good touches – Dad's hug when he tucks you in at night; Mom's kiss as you go out the door; the coach's slap on the back when he sends you into the game; a sister's hug when she discovers you've cleaned her room for her; Uncle Tom's hug and kiss when you meet him at the airport; Grandpa's hug when he says you are his number one granddaughter; your teammates' bear hugs when you hit a home run.

Bad touches – slaps, pinches, punches, hard hits on the head, kicks, hard swats, and spanks.

Confusing touches – tickling or wrestling that goes on for too long; touches on private parts of the body; being held on an adult's lap when you want down; kissing that is too long or too grown-up; overlong stroking of an arm or leg; any touches by a stranger or someone the child knows that seem *too* familiar.

Tell your kids it should be easy for them to understand the touches that are good and the ones that are bad. It's the uncomfortable and confusing touches that could be misunderstood. These are the ones you want to talk about. Tell your youngsters some of these confusing touches could be or could lead to sexual abuse, and you want them to know about it so that they won't be caught unaware if this ever happens to them. You want them prepared so that they will know how to deal with this type of uncomfortable touching.

Define sexual abuse or assault for your child. Many children imagine far worse things if they're not given an accurate, simple definition. Here's a definition you can use or put into your own words:

> Sexual assault is when an adult or older child touches areas of your body that are private (penis, vagina, anus— the private areas generally covered by a swimsuit). They might ask you to touch their private parts. They might ask you to take off your clothes, or they may undress in front of you. They may kiss you for a long time, or ask you to get in bed with them, or take pictures of you without your clothes. All this is considered sexual abuse or sexual assault, and we want to tell you about it so that you will know what to do if it ever happens to you.

When you discuss sexual assault with your children, try to avoid scaring them. There's no need to tell them details of a violent rape or an incestuous relationship: Don't go into the gory details even if they ask, but do try to answer their legitimate questions.

Tell them you're teaching them about sexual abuse because the situation is a possibility. It may never happen to them, but, like fire safety and first aid, we want to teach them what to do, just in case.

Some parents worry for fear their youngsters will begin to think every person they meet may be a sexual offender. To counter this concern, tell your children that people who are sexual offenders are the exception because most people respect and care about children's welfare and would not do anything to hurt them. Sexual offenders are disturbed or sick people in need of special help.

After defining sexual abuse, it's important to tell your children who might be a sexual abuser. Once again, tell them that most people are nice, and there are very few people who actually abuse children, but that *anyone* can be a potential abuser. Unfortunately, it is important for children to know that even people they trust and love may be potential sexual offenders. By telling children only about strangers who may be sexual offenders, we leave them unprotected against at least 85 percent of the potential sexual assaults. Kids need to know that the majority of assaults are committed by someone known to them—a teacher, an uncle, a baby-sitter, an older brother, a family friend, a neighbor, a coach, or even a parent. They need to know the truth: Most sexual assaults are not committed by strangers.

Tell your children they have the right to be the boss of their own bodies, including their private parts. No one should touch a child's private areas unless the child gives them permission to do so. (This is a good place to bring up the exceptions. A doctor or nurse may need to touch private areas during an examination or treatment; however, even medical personnel should ask permission.)

Tell your children that when someone touches them in a way that might be the beginning of a sexual abuse situation, they may experience a creepy, "yukky," or uncomfortable feeling that things are not all right. They should pay attention to those feelings. If you've discussed instinctive feelings (see page 186), they may already be aware of how important it is to listen to these messages, trust them, and take action to keep themselves safe.

Also tell your youngsters that when they feel uncomfortable about the way someone is touching them, or feel that it's wrong, they have the right to tell the person to stop. In fact, a simple, firm refusal is the strongest protection for any child, since the offender usually doesn't want the child to resist or raise a fuss. He usually leaves those youngsters alone for fear of exposure. After we've taught our children that they may refuse unwanted touches, it's important to teach them how to say no strongly and assertively. Here are a few pointers to teach your children.

1. Look the person straight in the eyes when you say no. Don't look down at your feet or glance away.

2. Stand up straight, with shoulders square and head up, when saying no.

3. Keep your facial expression serious: this means no smiling or laughing.

4. Make sure your refusal is firm. Use the word *no* rather than a weak phrase, such as "Oh, I'm not sure," "I don't really think I'd better," or "I don't think so."

5. Shake your head *no* to reinforce the verbal response.

6. You don't need to make up excuses; simply say no. Any excuse will give the person an opportunity to try to talk you into something. If the person keeps talking, you should just say no again. *A firm refusal leaves little room for argument.*

After we have given our youngsters permission to say no to touches they don't like, we must also respect them and be sure we do not try to force them into situations that may compromise their feelings. It may be embarrassing if they refuse a slobbery kiss from Grandpa or a suffocating hug from the lady down the street, but if the reasons for their refusal are explained, usually adults will be more understanding and supportive. Parents need to accept their youngsters' feelings and back them up. *If we don't, their ability to refuse unwanted touches will be weakened.*

You should tell your children that they should report any sexual abuse rather than keep it a secret, even if they have promised not to tell. Abusers often try to stop children from reporting the abuse by telling them the act will be a secret between the two of them. They often exact a promise the child will not tell. Make it clear to your children that these promises need not be kept, and that you need to know so you can stop the abuse and protect the child. Children who believe they will be backed up, listened to, and sheltered are more likely to report an incident.

Before you end your talk about sexual abuse, be sure to tell your youngsters that *it is never a child's fault if he or she is sexually abused.* The fault lies with the adult who instigated the assault. Since children very often feel a great deal of guilt in these situations, it is important to reassure them of their innocence. Tell them they are not at fault even if the sexual abuse went on a long time before they told someone about it. Also tell them that even if they said no and the abuse occurred anyway, it is not their fault because there are times when even a firm no will not stop an offender.

How to Reduce the Chance Your Child Will Be Sexually Abused

Parents can lessen the chance for sexual abuse to occur by setting limits for their children. Following the general safety rules presented in Chapter 10 of this book (go in a group, stay away from deserted areas, etc.) will reduce the possibility that your child will be assaulted by a stranger.

You can also lessen your children's chances of being sexually abused by someone you know by monitoring the adults who come into contact with your youngsters. Be wary of any adult who wants to spend time alone with a child for no apparent reason or shows an unusual interest in one child above the other youngsters. When your child complains about an adult, listen carefully to the complaint.

Try to screen those people who care for or come in contact with your children in your absence, such as baby-sitters, day-care workers, coaches, etc. Check with people who have used a certain baby-sitter or child-care worker, and talk with mothers whose children have been in contact with a coach. Ask your children how things went with a particular person, what they thought of him, and if they enjoyed being with him. Dropping in unexpectedly is also a good way to observe what's going on. Parents sometimes have an intuitive feeling that something is not quite right. If you get a funny feeling about a person or situation, listen to and respect those messages. If you don't completely trust the people with your child or feel uneasy about them, don't leave your youngster in their care.

I still remember the time I was going to take advantage of a baby-sitting service provided by people in a small town where several restored homes were on tour. When I saw the man who was going to supervise the youngsters, I had such an uneasy feeling that I decided to keep my daughters with me. Later on, I overheard two older women talking about how they couldn't understand the town hiring that man after he was forced to give up his Boy Scout group because of all the complaints. I never did learn whether the man deserved his poor reputation, but I have learned to trust my intuition and not take chances with my children. They're simply too precious.

Although sexual offenders look just like everyday folks, usually act normally, and may even be pillars of the community, most of them exhibit certain personality traits. Of course, many people with these same traits would never think of abusing a child, so you can't take these traits as conclusive evidence; but it won't hurt for you to be more cautious about your child's contact with people who display these characteristics.

1. People who relate to a child in a sexual manner; for example, someone who tells a little girl that she's a "sexpot" or a little boy that he's a real "hunk."

2. People who consistently entice children into their houses or into activities where parents are not present: for example, the track coach who wants to meet your child alone at the field or at his home for extra practice.

3. People who exhibit disrespect for a child by refusing to cease tickling, touching, kissing, or any other physical contact even after the child wants to stop.

4. People who you know were themselves abused as children.

5. People who are heavily involved in alcohol or drugs.

6. People who are from rigid, punitive backgrounds where sex was thought to be bad and dirty.

7. People who are loners.

8. People who relate more comfortably to children than to adults or their peers and who have no adult friends or confidants.

9. People who have been convicted of a previous sexual offense: Many psychologists believe sexual offenders cannot be completely cured.

If Your Child Has Been Assaulted

Often children do not tell about an assault in actual words because they may be embarrassed, or think it was their fault, or think they won't be believed, especially if the offender is known to the family. They may also be afraid to tell because of threats made to hurt them or members of their family if they disclose the assault. Even if children don't disclose an assault in words, they may communicate by behavior signals, and parents need to be aware of these signals. If you observe any of the following signs, find out what's going on with your child. Early discovery of sexual abuse can usually keep the problem from becoming even more serious.

1. The child may not want to be with a certain person. For example, a girl who liked her baby-sitter suddenly does not, or a boy who loved special outings with his uncle suddenly does not want to go with him.

2. The child may exhibit or describe sexual behavior inappropriate to his years and experience. Such behavior may include sexual posturing, french kissing, etc. It is possible the child may have picked up the information from peers or observed adult sexual behavior, but the knowledge may also have come from being victimized sexually.

3. A child may exhibit an *abnormal* interest in his own genitals, those of others, or even those of animals.

4. The child may have a sexually transmitted disease (gonorrhea, genital herpes, syphilis) that was caught from an adult or older child.

5. The child may have sleep disturbances—nightmares, trouble getting to sleep, or fear of the dark—which were not present before.

6. The child may be extremely irritable or withdrawn.

7. Teachers or day-care workers may notice a change in a child's habits, or a child may suddenly have difficulty concentrating.

8. The child may have pain during urination and defecation or discomfort in the genital area.

9. The child may show new fears and seem to need more reassurance than usual, may cling to parents and want to be held, may even return to babyish behavior such as talking baby talk or wetting his pants or bed.

10. The youngster may suddenly turn against one parent and be uncomfortable in that adult's presence.

11. An older child may begin self-destructive behavior such as drugs or alcohol, self-mutilation, attempted suicide, running away, promiscuity, or prostitution.

When You First Find Out about the Assault

Discovering a child has been assaulted is an overwhelming family crisis. No family can ever be totally prepared to cope with this disclosure. Although every situation is different, here are some suggestions that may help you deal with the crisis in a way that will not further traumatize your child.

1. Remain calm. When you learn your child has been sexually assaulted, your emotions are understandably in a turmoil. But it's very important for you to try to remain calm, and it is vital to your child that you do so.

2. Say you're glad the child told you. This will reassure the youngster that she did the right thing in disclosing the information. Children are often not really sure they should tell parents about a situation like this. The child may try to retract the telling if parents cannot control their first reaction to the news.

3. Direct your anger and rage. When parents learn their youngster has been sexually assaulted, they usually experience violent feelings of anger. These reactions are very natural, but it's vital that your child understands these feelings are directed at the offender, and not at her. You must emphasize that you are not angry at the child.

4. Ask questions gently. When your child first begins to talk about the assault, ask questions gently, but *don't pressure* the child to tell all the details right then. Be receptive and listen to what she says without forcing. If you need it, take a break to keep your own emotions under control.

5. Believe what you hear. Children very rarely make up stories about sexual assault, so it's important to believe what a child says. Many youngsters lack the vocabulary to describe the incident, but don't construe this lack of words or hesitation to mean that the story is made up. They may not be clear on details, time, or place, but they may remember more information later if they are not pressured.

6. Tell them it's not their fault. Since the majority of sexually abused children often assume a part or all of the blame, it's very important to emphasize that the assault was not the child's fault. Tell your child that the fault lies with the adult— he's the one who did wrong and is the one responsible.

7. Tell your child that the offender needs help. Many youngsters feel a great deal of guilt for bringing an assault to light, especially if it involves a close family member or trusted friend. They worry about breaking up the family or friendship. Parents can ease the child's fear by saying the offender needs help and will now get it because the situation was revealed. This thought often lifts the burden of guilt from the child.

8. Tell the child you are sorry about the incident. Although you cannot change what has already happened, you can show comfort and caring by saying you're sorry the incident happened. This sympathy and consolation communicates your care, love, and support to the youngster during this troubled time.

9. Communicate your protection. Let the child know you will protect her from the offender, especially if the abuser is a family member, but do not promise the abuser will be put in jail. Unfortunately we cannot always count on the criminal justice system to actually convict or incarcerate a sexual offender. Reassure your child that the incident is over, a thing of the past that will not happen again.

10. Consult a physician. Although you should always consult a doctor if the child has been raped or injured, it is also often comforting to have a doctor tell the child that everything is physically all right. If you take your child to a doctor, it's best if the physician is one the child knows, either the pediatrician or the family doctor or the mother's gynecologist. If that's not possible, take the child to the emergency room of your local hospital, and stay with her during the examination and any needed treatment. Be sure the child knows in words she can understand what's happening during an exam or treatment of the genital or rectal area. If the child has been raped, the examination can be used to document the injuries and sexual contact, collect evidence for court, check for and treat infection, and, in older girls, prevent pregnancy.

11. Get counseling for yourself. Most parents benefit from talking with someone who is experienced in dealing with sexual abuse situations. Good choices for assistance are family therapists or sexual assault centers where the staff are trained to help parents deal with sexual abuse.

12. Get counseling for the victim. Most experts believe therapy for the victim is not automatically necessary in child sexual abuse cases, but should be considered if the child is deeply troubled and unable to resolve her feelings. If your child does not seem to be returning to normal within a few months, or won't talk about the incident, or was abused by a family member, counseling should be considered. Family therapists, psychologists, psychiatrists, or sexual assault counselors who work with rape relief centers are all good choices. If the assault has been severe—a rape, for example—it's a good idea to get professional help for the youngster before the child reaches adolescence and begins to undergo the additional pressures of normal teenage turmoil. Counseling can help ensure a healthy attitude toward human sexuality in future years.

Reporting a Sexual Assault

After a child discloses an incident of sexual assault, parents must decide whether or not to report it to the authorities. There are no right or wrong answers to this difficult decision, but the most important consideration is to protect your child from further trauma. The following information may help you make this decision.

Parents fear that their child may suffer more trauma as a witness involved in the legal process than as a victim of the assault. They are concerned that the reporting, investigation, and possible trial appearances may further endanger the child's mental health by forcing the youngster to repeatedly face traumatic memories of the assault. They worry that insensitive and untrained personnel may further traumatize the youngster, and they also feel powerless to protect their child from an inconsistent and often callous legal intervention system.

However, many courts have recently taken dramatic steps to make the legal process far less stressful and more compassionate for child victims of sexual assault. It is also important that parents realize that the reporting and follow-up involvement in the legal process may actually be beneficial to child victims. When children find they *do* have power within the legal system to stop the abuse, when they discover that society *does* believe them and will protect them, the entire process may be a catharsis.

Parents may think the sexually abused child is too young to testify about the incident. Generally, children 5 years and older who can remember what happened and can talk about it can be competent witnesses. When children are younger, physical evidence of the abuse may be sufficient. If the offender has disclosed the assault to a psychiatrist, psychologist, or counselor, such evidence is not protected and can be used in court.

When the abuser is a family member, there is usually a greater reluctance to report the crime and face possible prosecution, since prosecution of a family member, particularly a father, is likely to have negative consequences for the entire family. Although the child and other family members want the abuse stopped, they are often economically dependent upon the offender, love him, and want the family to remain intact. The parents or parent reporting the incident may feel guilty about accusing a family member and may fear hostility and rejection from the rest of the family for exposing the taboo.

A mother may hesitate to report an incident of incest because she wants to protect her husband. She may not want it to appear that she made a poor choice in a mate or that her sexual inadequacies somehow drove her husband to commit the abuse. However, a mother has the greater responsibility to protect her children from harm.

Parents may be reluctant to expose an incident because they think their child may be lying. If the offender is a trusted family friend, parents may believe the friend rather than their child, even though it has been proven that children rarely lie about an incident of sexual assault. No more than two or three children per thousand exaggerate or invent claims of sexual abuse, and these rare fabrications are usually quickly brought to light.

Parents may mistakenly believe the offender when he pleads he will not repeat the crime. However, it is almost certain he will repeat his behavior if nothing is done to stop him. Many adult sexual offenders report assaulting as many as 100 different children over a period of years, and many offenders within the family may assault successive generations of youngsters if they are not stopped by authorities.

Some parents want to keep the incident of sexual assault private and handle it themselves. They may distrust law enforcement or judicial agencies or feel shame and embarrassment about reporting such a personal incident. But most parents do not have the experience or authority to handle an incident of sexual assault on their own. In many areas, police and judicial personnel have received special training to help them deal with sexual assault victims and families sensitively and compassionately.

Parents may not report the assault because they want the child to forget the incident as quickly as possible and get on with life. They feel the less they dwell on the assault the quicker the child will forget it, too. But trying to forget the incident will not stop the offender from molesting, and most children do not quickly forget the assault.

Evaluating the Criminal Justice Process

Parents who are considering whether or not to report a sexual assault and submit a child to the criminal justice process can phone their local prosecutor's office and ask what procedures are followed when a case of sexual abuse is prosecuted in their area. Parents can often get an idea of whether the system seems sympathetic and supportive of the child victim or not. The following are some of the recent changes that have been made in legal systems to make the prosecution of sexual offense much less stressful for the child victim.

1. Some districts staff their sexual assault programs with professionals who are trained in child development, the effects of child sexual abuse, and techniques for reducing the stress on the child victim. Often the same personnel may handle a case all the way through the criminal justice process.

2. Some criminal justice systems have been modified to reduce the number of times a child victim has to be interviewed. Joint interviews with various agencies are conducted, or the interview may be videotaped. Efforts are made to make the child feel comfortable by using interview rooms which may resemble colorful playrooms complete with toys and child-size furniture. Interviewers first try to get to know the child and chat about nonthreatening subjects before gradually introducing the subject of the assault. Youngsters may use anatomically correct dolls to show what happened instead of having to relate it verbally.

3. If the case goes to trial, many prosecutors make sure the child is given a preliminary tour of the courtroom, along with an explanation of who will be there (judges, attorneys, jury, etc.) and what will happen during the trial.

4. Sometimes alternatives to actual court appearances may be used such as indictments obtained on the basis of the child's out-of-court deposition. An increasing number of states allow the testimony of children to be given via closed-circuit television so that the youngster does not have to face a courtroom full of spectators, the defendant, bailiffs, court reporters, and others.

5. There is an increasing emphasis on making sure that children are questioned at their own level with words and phrases they understand so they don't have to answer questions they may not fully comprehend. Often the court uses the child's own words for body parts. Although the purpose of cross-examination by the defense attorney is to cast doubt on the child's competence or truthfulness, an effort is made to shield the youngster from abusive cross-examination.

Two Methods of Reporting the Incident

Parents who decide to report a sexual abuse incident have two choices as to how the report is made. A report can be made anonymously through an agency such as a rape relief center or child protective services agency. In this case the police can use the information given, but no further investigation will be made, and little or nothing will be done to stop the abuser. The second choice is to make a report directly to the police. In this case, a police officer will arrive to provide immediate assistance and protection, make an initial crime report, and collect evidence. Usually a detective assigned to the case will follow up with further investigations.

Activities for Practice

Man in the Theater

Set up two chairs side by side. The parent takes the role of a man who sits down next to the child in a crowded theater and puts his hand on the child's leg. Ask your child what she will do. Ask her what she will do if the man does not stop.

Teenage Baby-Sitter

Play the role of a teenage baby-sitter who asks your child to take off all his clothes so the two of you can play a very special secret game. Tell the child he gets to watch a late TV show if he plays the game. If he says no, tell him you are going to report he was a bad boy when his parents get home. Can your child keep on saying no?

Family Friend

Role-play the part of a family friend who wants to take some pictures. Tell your child her body is beautiful and natural and you want to take pictures of her without her clothes. Bribe the youngster with the offer of money, etc. See how she copes with this situation.

What-If Games

Ask your youngsters what they would do in these situations.

   1. What if Grandpa kept on touching the youngster's private parts during a tickling session?

2. What if her piano teacher repeatedly stroked the back of her neck during a private music lesson?

3. What if an adult at the day-care center told him to undress and tried to touch his private parts?

4. What if an adult in a public bathroom offered the child $10 to touch the adult's private parts?

5. What if her stepfather gave her a long, deep, sloppy, "romantic" kiss when he tucked her in at night? What if she told her stepfather to stop, but he would not?

6. What if a friend of the family showed the child a "bad" (sexually explicit) movie and made the youngster promise not to tell?

7. What if he were alone at the park and a stranger came up and showed his penis?

8. What if your child told an adult about a sexual assault and the adult did not believe her?

9. What if his best friend revealed he was being sexually abused by an uncle?

10. What if someone had sexually abused her and then told her that he would kill her dog if she ever told anyone about the assault?

Questions to Ask Your Child

Ask your children these questions to see if they have understood.

1. Who would you go to for help if you had been sexually abused? What would you do if the person you asked for help did not believe you?

2. What would you do if you had promised to keep an incident of sexual assault a secret? Would you tell, and why?

3. What types of people could possibly abuse youngsters sexually?

4. What are some examples of good touches, bad touches, and confusing touches?

5. What would you do if you hated Grandma's sloppy, long kisses, but you don't want to hurt her feelings?

6. Who is in charge of your body?

7. Is there anyone who can touch your private parts?

8. Are most sexual abusers strangers?

9. Show how you would say no assertively.

10. What body language makes a refusal more assertive?

In Conclusion

While parents cannot completely protect their children from the possibility of sexual assault, we can help greatly by teaching our youngsters about this problem and instructing them how to avoid it. We can also keep communication lines open so that our youngsters feel free to discuss this subject with us and get help if it should happen to them. Parents need to be aware that children do not always disclose a sexual assault in words, but they may evince by their behavior that something is wrong. If a child is assaulted, parents must know where to get help and be aware of what can be expected when the incident is reported.

Chapter 9

KEEPING YOUR CHILDREN BUSY

We've long been told that idle hands are the devil's workshop, while a song popular when my oldest was born says of children, "You don't need direction. You know which way to go. I'm not going to stop you. I just want to watch you grow." Who is right? Should we keep our children so busy they don't have a spare minute, or should we leave their hours completely unstructured?

Most parents lean toward structuring a good part of their children's free time with planned activities in hopes the youngsters will not be bored or, far worse, tempted into undesirable activities such as taking drugs, sexual experimentation, and the like. Whether you decide to fill most of your child's free time or only provide occasional activities, this chapter will help you keep your children busy.

Supplies to Keep Kids Busy

To help keep your kids busy, it's a good idea to have the following supplies on hand.

1. Pencils, pens, crayons, white and colored chalk, colored pencils, and colored felt-tip marking pens.

2. Paints: water colors, tempera paints, fingerpaints, and assorted brushes.

3. Paper: colored construction paper, block graph paper, tracing paper, drawing paper, lined paper, tissue paper, and crêpe paper.

4. Scissors.

5. Clay or homemade play dough and baker's clay (sometimes called sculptor's clay).

RECIPE FOR PLAY DOUGH

1½ cups flour
½ cup salt
½ cup water
¼ cup vegetable oil
few drops of food coloring

Mix the flour and salt in a pan or bowl. Add the water slowly, then add the oil and food coloring. Knead the dough well. Store in refrigerator in a tightly covered container or a plastic bag. If the dough is sticky, add more flour.

RECIPE FOR BAKER'S CLAY

2 cups flour
½ cup salt
¾ cup hot water

Mix the flour and salt together. Add the hot water, and knead the mixture well. This is a stiff dough that can be used for making figures and ornaments. Objects can be baked in a conventional oven at 200 degrees Fahrenheit for at least an hour or until hard and dry. When objects have cooled, they can be painted.

6. Glue or paste, masking tape, clear scotch tape (keep superglue or crazy glue away from children).

7. String, yarn, ribbon, thread, and large-eyed needles.

8. Milk cartons, cardboard tubes from paper towels and bathroom tissue, boxes of any size, from tiny cartons to huge packing crates.

9. Paper bags of all sizes, from sandwich size to grocery bag size (make sure children do not use dangerous plastic bags).

10. Toothpicks, paper clips, rubber bands, empty thread spools, pipe cleaners, etc.

11. Old scrap lumber and pieces of wood for indoor construction projects or outdoor activities.

12. Odds and ends such as clean bottles, corks, jars, cans, etc.

13. Old clothes, hats, shoes, and accessories for dress up and dramatic play.

Also fun and useful are craft kits, such as simple looms and sewing or needlecraft projects, and simple model kits for cars, boats, planes, and the like that can be constructed without much adult supervision. You can pick up inexpensive puzzles, board games, and hobby kits at garage sales and thrift stores run by the Salvation Army, Goodwill, and St. Vincent de Paul; occasionally you can even get construction sets such as Lincoln Logs, Legos, Tinker Toys, Erector Sets, Bristle Blocks, wooden or plastic blocks, and wooden train sets. To keep a supply of "new" board games, some families trade games every so often. Kits, games, and construction sets all stimulate creative imagination and are fun for youngsters of all ages.

If you allow your children to play outdoors when they are home alone, the very best outdoor object is a simple dirt pile or sandbox. Add a few toy cars, scraps of wood, a little imagination, and children will occupy themselves for hours.

Things to Do

When your youngsters complain that they have nothing to do, refer them to the following list of kid-tested activities.

40 Indoor Activities

1. Make a necklace by threading round cereal such as Cheerios. See how long a necklace you can make, then eat it (but don't eat the thread!).

2. Play Post Office with the discarded junk mail your family receives. Make mailboxes from shoe boxes by covering them with construction paper or aluminum foil.

3. Pretend you're shopping from a catalog (Sears, Wards, etc.) for an entire new school wardrobe. Don't forget to pick out socks and shoes, too. If it's all right with your parents, fill out the order form, price everything, list the pounds and ounces, colors and sizes. Or pick out toys for yourself or a friend, brother, or sister from a Christmas catalog. Remember this is just pretend; don't mail the order form!

4. Have a straw-and-marble race. Move your marble by blowing on it through a straw. See how fast you can go, or set up a special course and see if you can blow your marble through it.

5. Improve your memory! Put various items (at least twenty different things) on a tray. Look at them for one minute, then cover the tray. On a piece of paper list how many items you can remember. Then uncover the tray, and see which ones you forgot. Try again until you can remember every single item. You can play this game alone or with a friend.

6. Pretend you're an actor doing a television commercial. Hold up your product, and practice what you'll say in front of a mirror. If your parents have a tape recorder they will let you use, record your commercial.

7. Play library. Put your own books in alphabetical order or according to subject matter, and make play library cards. Be the librarian, and try to help your patrons choose a book.

8. Get brochures of exciting places from a travel agent, and plan where you'll go on a pretend trip. You can also play Travel Agent, and help your customers plan their world cruise or expensive vacation.

9. Have a tea party with your dolls. Get them all dressed up, put them on their best behavior, and let them sit at a special table you have set.

10. Get car brochures from new-car dealers. Cut out cars you like, or pretend you are selling a car to a customer.

11. Make up a newspaper telling about people in your class at school and the subjects you are studying. Or make a newspaper for your family or neighborhood telling about recent happenings. If it is possible for parents to make copies of your newspaper, give a copy to family members or neighbors.

12. Write a letter to a friend using invisible ink. Either make a quill pen out of a feather, or use a paper clip, toothpick, or old pen that is out of ink. Write with lemon juice, white vinegar, or even milk. Have your friend heat the letter over a lightbulb until the writing shows.

13. Pretend to be a secretary, banker, office manager, etc., with receipt books or old office forms provided by your parents.

14. Make up a play. Get your friends to help, and put the play on for your parents. Or put on a puppet show. Make puppets from small paper bags. Cut eyes, mouth, hair, and eyelashes from construction paper, and glue it on the bag. Use an empty cardboard box for a stage, and practice acting out the puppet show.

15. Find out how to play the card game solitaire. Maybe your parents would buy you a paperback book that lists 100 ways to play solitaire.

16. Write a surprise letter to Grandma, Grandpa, Aunt, Uncle, or your cousin. If there is an old typewriter in your home, ask your parents if you may use it. Or ask your school or public librarian for names of pen pals you can write to.

17. Play with paper dolls, or make your own by cutting a figure out of a magazine; then draw and cut out clothes for your figure.

18. Ask parents to save empty food boxes and cans. When you get enough, set up a store. Put prices on your items and make play money to use.

19. Play school with a friend, or if you are alone, set up your dolls or stuffed animals as students, and see how smart they are.

20. See if you can find a radio schedule in your newspaper. Mark any good radio dramas or music programs that will be on at the times when you are alone.

21. Do a jigsaw puzzle. If it is an easy one that you have done before, time yourself to see how long it takes to put it together; then try it again, and see if you can improve your time.

22. Read a magazine or trade magazines with a friend. Ask neighbors to save good magazines for you. You could even collect old magazines to take to a senior center or nursing home in your area.

23. If you can use a phonograph, play records. See if your public library has records you can check out and listen to at home. Perhaps you could ask parents to buy a Souza march record for you so you could practice marching through the house and keeping time to the music. Or put on a music record, and pretend you are the conductor leading the orchestra.

24. Line up all your stuffed animals. Pretend you are a veterinarian, and treat their ills. Bandage their sprained legs with paper towels and tape, and put the sick ones tenderly to bed.

25. Make up a secret code. When you get it perfected, show a friend so that you can exchange secret messages.

26. Clean out and rearrange a family coat closet. Hang up all the coats and sweaters, sort out mittens, find mates to the boots, fold scarfs and caps, and stand umbrellas in a large empty coffee can in the corner of the closet.

27. Try to memorize five letters of Morse code. Test yourself to be sure you can remember them. Your public or school library will have books about Morse code.

28. Draw a map of your neighborhood. Mark friends' homes and stores, and show your route to school. Or draw a plan of your yard and put in all the changes you would make if you could. If you live in an apartment, draw a plan of your dream yard.

29. Look at hair styles in a magazine or in the newspaper ads; then see if you can arrange your own or a friend's hair that way. No cutting or hair coloring, please!

30. Start a journal or diary. Write it with the idea that many years from now people may want to know what it was like to be a child in the 1980s. Describe the tools you use, the games you play, the things you study in school, and the clothes you wear.

31. Line up your cars, airplanes, dolls, model horses, or other toys, and have a show. Make ribbons out of paper. If you have model horses, set up a jump course for them, using blocks or Lincoln Logs. Use small mirrors to simulate water jumps, and award paper ribbons to your winners.

32. Plan a neighborhood carnival or talent show. If you can have friends over, ask them to help you. Set a date, practice your acts, make up programs, and hold the carnival. Or have a magic show. Get a book on magic tricks from your library, practice a few stunts until you get good, and put on a show for your friends and family.

33. Write a story, draw pictures to illustrate it, then make it into a book by poking holes along the left side or top of the pages and tying them together with string, yarn, or ribbon. These books can make special gifts.

34. Ask for old wallpaper books at a paint store, and make things with the paper samples. You can make greeting cards, doll clothes, houses, and other things. You can also play Wallpaper Store and help your pretend customers pick out wallpaper for rooms in their homes.

35. Cut out pictures of your dream room or dream home from magazines and catalogs. Choose the furniture, curtains, bed spread, paint, wallpaper, and carpets. Or using graph paper, draw a houseplan for your dream home.

36. Make up a new dance. Practice it while looking in a mirror.

37. Keep a log of the time the street lights go on each evening to see if the days are really getting shorter or longer.

38. Put a marshmallow in a spoon, and see how fast you can walk without it falling out; or try balancing an old book on your head, and see how far you can walk before the book slips off.

39. Put a page from an old calendar on the floor or counter, and toss buttons or pennies onto it. You score if your penny lands on a numbered day of the month—the higher the day of the month, the higher your score. If the penny is half on and half off, you get another try. Add up your score by adding the numbers you land on. The game is over when you reach a total of 150 points. Time yourself to see how long it takes you to reach that score.

40. If parents have an exercise bike they will let you ride, see how long it takes you to ride 1 mile; then try it again, and see if you can beat your time.

18 Art Activities

1. Put some runny paint on paper, and blow through a straw onto the paint to make a special design.

2. Bend pipe cleaners or wire to make the shapes of animals, flowers, or human figures.

3. Collect your best pictures, or create others for an art show. Frame your best work with construction paper strips, write your name and the title of the picture on a piece of paper, and ask permission to put the works on a wall at home.

4. Scribble lines all over a paper. Turn the paper sideways and upside-down to see if you can imagine pictures or forms from the lines. Color in any forms you see, or just color shapes at random.

5. Write your name with paint on one end of a piece of paper. While the paint is still wet, fold the paper together with the name inside and rub the folded paper gently. When you open it up, your name should be duplicated in reverse on the other side of the paper.

6. With play dough or modeling clay, make figures for a zoo or dishes, foods, and plates for a pretend restaurant. Or make figures to act out your favorite story.

7. Draw a forest scene freehand, or trace a picture in a magazine.

8. Ask your parents or teacher what a collage is. Get some stiff paper or cardboard, cut out pictures from old magazines, and paste them on the paper. Choose pictures that tell about you or your interests. Or make a collage for a friend that shows the things he or she is interested in.

9. Ask if you can have macaroni, rice, and several types of beans and pastas. Decide on a design, then glue these foods onto stiff paper or cardboard.

10. With firm paper and a felt-tip pen, make a decorative sign with your name on it. Ask parents if you can tape it up somewhere inside your house.

11. Make a mosaic. Ask your parents to save empty egg shells and an egg carton for you. Crush a couple of shells into each section of the empty egg carton, add a few drops of different paint to each section, and mix it with the crushed shells. Draw a design on paper with a pencil or pen. Smear glue on one section of the design, and sprinkle your crushed colored egg shells over the glue. Let that area dry, then continue with the next section until your design is finished.

12. With permission, draw on the sidewalk or driveway with colored chalk. Draw houses and roads, and play with your cars. Or draw a pretty scene or flowers. When it's time to clean up, take a broom and hose, and scrub the chalk away.

13. Make rubbings of various things such as leaves, coins, pebbly concrete, and the like. Put a piece of paper over the surface, and rub lightly with pencil, crayon, or chalk. You will see the print or rubbing of the surface you chose.

14. Draw mustaches, beards, and hair on the faces of people pictured in a newspaper or magazine your parents have already read. Make one character look mean, another look surprised, another happy, and another sad.

15. Draw triangles, squares, swirls, and circles on an old board. Collect small pebbles, and glue them to the various forms to make a mosaic. Your finished artwork can be hung out of doors on a garage wall, an inside wall, a fence, or the deck of your apartment building.

16. Make a mobile of shells, pieces of driftwood, nuts, and various dried pastas such as macaroni, shell macaroni, bundles of spaghetti, or ricotta noodles. Use a wire clothes hanger for the main part, and tie various lengths of string to it; then tie or glue your objects on the string.

17. Glue rocks together to form imaginary creatures, and then paint their faces and hair or fur. Put rocks and sand in the top of a shoe box to create a "moonscape," and put your rock creatures in it.

18. Paint faces or scenes on flat rocks, and use them for paperweights. Give the nicest ones to your parents to use at work or at home.

20 Nature Activities

1. Make a potpourri, a mixture of dry flower petals kept for their fragrance. Gather fragrant wild or garden flowers, cut them in small pieces, and let them dry in the sun. When they are dry, tie them in squares of cloth or netting, and put them in closets and drawers. You can also store the potpourri in jars. Potpourri gives off a lovely scent and makes nice gifts.

2. Blindfold a friend, and take him on a mixed-up route to a certain tree or shrub in your yard or the park. (Make sure you have permission to go to the park.) Ask him to feel the leaves, bark, and any exposed roots and smell the tree for any distinctive odor. Then take him back to the starting point, remove the blindfold, and ask him to figure out which tree he touched just by remembering what he observed when he was blindfolded.

3. Make spore prints of mushrooms. Gather mushrooms, but be sure not to eat any. Take off the cap (top), and put it gill-side down on a piece of paper; try both light and dark construction paper. Cover it with a bowl, and leave it overnight. Remove the cap the next day to see the print the mushroom left. The print won't smudge if you spray it lightly with hairspray, and you can use this spore-printed paper as stationery.

4. Get a book about trees from your school or public library. See if you can identify any of the trees in your neighborhood. Gather leaves from different trees, bring them inside, lay them out, and see if you can identify the tree just by the leaves. In the fall, with permission, pick branches of brilliantly colored foliage, put them in a vase, and enjoy the autumn colors. See if your book tells why leaves change color in the autumn. You can also put the colorful leaves between sheets of waxed paper. With your parents' help, press the waxed paper with an iron set on "warm." Frame the "picture" with strips of construction paper, and put it in a window where light can shine through.

5. Make homemade sprouts with dry beans such as lima beans. Lay a jar on its side and line it with paper towels; put the beans between the towels and the side of the jar so that you can see what happens. Now put some water in the bottom of the jar, and add a bit more each day to keep the paper towel moist. Put the jar in a sunny window, and watch the beans sprout after a few days. You can eat the sprouts by themselves, use them in a salad, or put them on sandwiches.

6. Have someone save styrofoam egg cartons for you. Fill each hole with good soil, and plant one or two flower or vegetable seeds in the soil. Lightly water the soil, then place the cartons in a sunny window. Keep a written record of when the first seeds sprout and appear, how many come up in one week, how many come up in two weeks, and so on. When the weather is warmer, your plants can be carefully transplanted to the ground outside. If you live in an apartment, transplant them to a larger pot, and keep it in a sunny window.

7. Ask your parents if you can have space in your yard for your very own garden. Dig up the soil, get rid of the weeds, then plant seeds or small vegetable or flower starts. If you live in an apartment, perhaps your landlord would let you garden in a small outdoor space.

8. Get a bird book from your school or public library, and see if you can identify the birds in your neighborhood. Ask your parents if you can put out food for the birds. Birds especially like slices of bread spread with peanut butter or pieces of suet tied in bushes or trees. Put out a shallow pan or bowl of cool water for birds to use as a bird bath. Put bits of string, cotton, or lint from the dryer on the grass or on low tree branches in the spring when you see birds looking for nesting material. Then watch from a distance to see if they take it. If you live in an apartment, ask parents for permission to do this at a nearby park with a friend.

9. See if your school or public library has a book about insects. If you find dead bugs, you can start a bug collection of your own. Mount the insects by pinning or gluing them to stiff paper. The top of a cardboard shoe box is an ideal display board for your collection. Using the book, see if you can identify the bugs and label each specimen.

10. Ask parents for a spare bowl or dish to use for a dish garden. Plant small weeds or mosses in the bowl to look like miniature trees and bushes, add small rocks or dirt, and sprinkle the dish garden with water. Small figurines or tiny toys look nice in a dish garden.

11. Indoors or outdoors, lie quietly and count the different sounds you hear. How many are natural sounds, such as birds or wind, and how many sounds are made by machines, such as subways and cars?

12. Dig up earthworms, put them in a very large jar with some of the soil you found them in, and give them a bit of water and some decaying leaves to eat. Watch them for a week to see the tunnels they make, then put them back where you found them. Don't forget to lightly cover the worms so a passing bird doesn't make a meal of them.

13. Start a rock collection, and see how many different kinds of rocks you can find. Check out a book on rocks from your school or public library, and see if you can identify any of the specimens in your collection.

14. Start plants from common fruits and vegetables. Plant apple, orange, and grapefruit seeds from fruit your family has eaten, and see if they sprout. Stick toothpicks into three sides of avocado pits or sweet potatoes to suspend them part way in a jar of water until they sprout. Carrot tops often grow if you cut off the top inch of a carrot and put it in a water-filled saucer.

15. Make a flower arrangement in a pretty vase or glass. Buy the flowers, use some from your yard (with permission), or pick pretty weed flowers. You can also add leaves, grasses, or other natural material to your arrangement and use it for a table centerpiece.

16. String shells, seed pods, or other natural things you find into a bracelet or necklace. Pick some large flower blossoms such as rhododendrons—with permission, of course—and string them into lovely leis.

17. Arrange flowers or leaves between sheets of newspaper, put the sheets between book pages, and pile heavy books on top to press them down. After two weeks, take out the pressed flowers and leaves, and glue them to nice paper for use as special stationery or bookmarks.

18. See how many different weeds you can find in your yard or, with parents' permission, around your neighborhood. Bring in a sample of each one, and try to draw it on paper.

19. Find some slugs or snails, and have a race! Draw a chalk circle in the shade on the sidewalk or driveway. Put the creatures in the circle, and see which one can get out of the circle first. Don't forget to put all winners and losers back where you found them.

20. Cut a citrus fruit such as orange, lime, lemon, or grapefruit in half between the stem and bud ends. Dip the cut half into paint and press it onto paper to make a pattern of the fruit. You can make special stationery or cards from your prints.

16 Outdoor or Physical Activities

1. If it is hot outdoors, run through the sprinkler, or, with your parents' permission, make a water slide by putting large plastic leaf bags on the lawn. Run water from a hose over the bags to make them slippery. Have fun, but remember to pick them up as soon as you're through, or they may damage the lawn.

2. Ask your librarian for a book on children's games. Play some of the ones that are new to you or your friends.

3. Make (but do not eat) pretend foods from dirt, leaves, flower petals, berries, bark, seeds, and such. Set up a pretend delicatessen or fast-food restaurant for your goodies.

4. With your parents' permission, set up a lemonade stand in your neighborhood, and sell cool drinks to friends and neighbors. Be sure you practice cleanliness by using a clean paper cup or glass for every customer and cleaning up any litter.

5. Make a pretend camp with old blankets. Gather rocks to make a fire ring and put sticks inside, but do not light your fire. If you can't go outside, make a pretend camp in your apartment or house.

6. Have a treasure hunt for friends or family. Make each clue lead to the next one until the treasure is discovered. For example, give your hunters a piece of paper with the clue "Look at the west corner of the shed." Then hide the next clue at the west corner of the shed and have it point to another place where the next clue will be found. The treasure could be a candy bar or cookies. You can also arrange a treasure hunt indoors if you cannot go outside.

7. After a rain, float leaves on the puddles. Pretend your leaves are boats. If you choose different kinds of leaves, they can represent boats from different navys, and you can stage battles or have boat races.

8. With parents' permission, go on a neighborhood litter patrol. Carry a paper bag to collect litter. Be sure you dispose of it properly.

9. If you are lucky enough to have an outdoor basketball hoop, shoot some baskets. Time yourself to see how many baskets you can make in two minutes.

10. With permission, draw a hopscotch course with chalk on the sidewalk or driveway. Draw a really long, challenging one.

11. Toss a ball or (indoors) a balloon, and see how many times you can catch it without missing.

12. Outdoors or indoors, set up an exercise or obstacle course, and see how long it takes you to go through it.

13. Roll down a safe, grassy hill. Be sure to brush yourself off before you go back in your house or apartment.

14. Play with cars in a sandbox, or dirt pile. Make roads, bridges, tunnels, and the like. If you can't be out of doors, see if you can make "roads" on your carpeting by simply rubbing the nap the wrong way with your fingers.

15. Time yourself to see how long it takes to walk around your block. Time yourself running or skipping around the block. See if you can beat your own time.

16. Buy a jar of bubble soap and blow bubbles, or make your own by putting 2 tablespoons of liquid soap in 1 cup of water and dipping your bubble maker in that. See how many bubbles you can blow with just one breath.

28 Seasonal and Holiday Activities

JANUARY

1. If there is snow where you live, make an entire family of snow people. With permission, dress your characters in old clothes. See if you can make snow animals like dogs, cats, or horses. Making snow forts or houses is also fun; after you've made them and stockpiled snowballs, challenge other neighborhood kids to a friendly snowball fight.

2. If Jack Frost left frost scenes on your windowpanes, see if you can copy his patterns on paper. You can make similar frost patterns with your fingerpaints, using toothpicks or combs to draw the intricate frost lines.

3. With permission, plan the table decorations for a special January dinner. Make place cards out of white paper decorated with small snowflakes you have cut, and write the person's name on the card. Make snowmen for a centerpiece from marshmallows held together by toothpicks. Decorate your snowmen with eyes, mouth, nose, and buttons cut from small pieces of felt or paper and glued to the marshmallow faces.

VALENTINE'S DAY

4. Make a Valentine's Day tree hung with red hearts. If your parents will let you cut some bare branches from shrubs or trees, put sand or rocks around the branches to anchor them in a vase or jar. Cut hearts out of red, pink, and white construction paper. Glue both ends of a short piece of string to the heart, let dry, then loop the string over the branches. You could even write little love messages on the hearts and use the tree for a table decoration.

5. Make your own valentines. First put down newspaper to work on, then assemble scissors, tape, glue or paste, construction paper, paints, paper doilies, aluminum foil, bits of ribbon, and so on. Fold paper into cards and decorate with hearts, doilies, and anything else that looks nice. Draw or paint decorations, then write poems or messages inside the valentines.

6. Save the valentine cards you receive, and have a card shop. Line up all the valentines, and pretend you are the clerk helping people choose special cards for their family or friends.

SPRING AND EASTER

7. Ask a parent to show you how to poke holes in eggs with needles and blow the egg out. Save the yolk and white for cakes or scrambled eggs. Wash out the shells, and carefully paint them for Easter. You can paint spring scenes or flowers or whatever you want. Coloring hard-boiled eggs is also fun, but be sure to have a parent's help with that project.

8. This month or next you can force-bloom branches from flowering trees or shrubs. With permission, cut some branches, bring them indoors and put them in a vase or jar of water. After a week or more they will usually begin to leaf out and bloom in the warm indoors. Use your branches for an arrangement or table centerpiece.

ST. PATRICK'S DAY

9. Look for four-leaf clovers around your yard or in a nearby park. How many can you find? How about five-leaf clovers? Press them between newspaper and the pages of a heavy book. After a few days they will be ready to glue onto construction paper for St.Patrick's Day cards. You can also put them between two sheets of waxed paper and, with parents' permission, lightly iron the paper with an iron set on low.

MAY DAY

10. Surprise your family and friends with a May basket on the first of May. Hang it on their door, ring the doorbell, and

run and hide. You can make the basket out of construction paper, decorate it with pretty ribbon scraps, and fill it with flowers
that are blooming in your yard, pretty weeds and leaves, or store-
bought flowers. You can also make paper flowers out of colored
tissues or even individual sheets of toilet tissue. Stack up about
ten sheets. Pinch the stacked sheets in the middle to make a place
where you can attach the stem. Wrap a wire or pipe cleaner
around the pinch to make a stem. This pinch should make the
top of the tissues fan out like a flower. Trim the flower part if
you want to make it smaller. To make a daisylike flower, cut many
slits in the top to look like petals. You can even dab on some
paint or color the flower with felt-tip markers.

FOURTH OF JULY

11. Decorate your wagon or bike with red, white, and blue
crepe paper for the Fourth of July, or draw and color a picture
of the United States flag and hang it in your window. If your
town or city has a parade, see if kids can march or ride bikes in
it.

SEPTEMBER

12. In your yard, rake the fallen leaves into piles and jump
in them or bury yourself or a friend. Do not make piles of leaves
in the street because children have been hurt by cars pulling away
from the curb. Then rake the leaves into outlines for roads, houses, etc. Afterwards, put them in plastic leaf bags, and tie the bags
so they can go out with the garbage pickup.

OCTOBER AND HALLOWEEN

13. Ask a friend over to "feel" some ghoulish monster parts.
Blindfold your friend and ask him to touch peeled grapes or
plums (monster eyeballs), cold cooked spaghetti rinsed with cold
water (monster blood veins or hair), rubber gloves filled with cold
water (monster hands), a small bowl of catsup (blood), and so
on.

14. If parents have a tape recorder, record your own spooky
sounds. Horrible screams will upset the neighbors, but maybe

you can rattle chains, moan and groan, and rattle cookie sheets to sound like thunder. Use your imagination.

15. If Mom has old makeup she will let you use, make your face scary for Halloween.

16. Make a Halloween mask by decorating a large grocery bag. Use scissors to cut out holes for eyes and mouth; then curl ribbon, or use cut yarn for hair.

17. Decorate a pumpkin. Instead of cutting out the face with a knife, draw or paint it on, and use a hat or a wig to complete your character.

THANKSGIVING

18. Ask your librarian for books on the Pilgrims so that you can find out how they lived. Pretend you are a Pilgrim child, and write a story about how you celebrated the first Thanksgiving in the New World.

19. Make construction-paper turkeys. First spread your fingers and trace around your hand. Your thumb will be the turkey's head, and your four fingers will be the feathers. Cut bright-colored paper to fit over the feathers, and color in the turkey's features. Mount the turkeys on brown construction paper, and use them as placemats for your Thanksgiving table.

CHRISTMAS AND HANUKKAH

20. Make a Christmas or Hanukkah tree for the birds. Hang suet, popcorn chains, or pine cones covered with peanut butter and bird seed on the branches of an outdoor tree, and watch the birds come for a holiday dinner.

21. Find out holiday traditions in other countries, and, with permission, incorporate one of them into your own family holiday celebration.

22. To practice the true meaning of the holiday season, which is giving to others, go through your old toys and clothes to find things you can donate to families who are less fortunate than yours. Make sure parents approve your donations. Call your fire station or police department to find out where you can drop off these holiday gifts.

23. Ask your parents for a knife that isn't too sharp. Use it to carve a pattern in a potato half. Dip the carved half in paint, and press it onto paper to duplicate the pattern. If you cut the shape of a tree, a bell, or a candle and press the pattern onto red or green paper, you can make Hanukkah or Christmas cards.

24. Make snowflakes by folding a square paper in half, then in half again, then cutting many pieces out of it. When you unfold it you will see a snowflake pattern. Glue snowflakes on dark-colored paper to use for special winter placemats, or tape your creations to a window.

25. With permission, plan a caroling party and invite your friends. Plan the menu (cookies would be a good treat if you are allowed to use the stove). Sing Christmas carols or Hanukkah songs to neighbors, and come back to your place for refreshments.

26. Make a nativity scene with play dough or baker's clay, and set it up on a special tray or cookie sheet covered with foil. Act out the story of Christ's birth.

27. Make napkin rings from play dough or baker's clay. Make tree or bell shapes, put rings on the back to hold the napkins, and let them dry thoroughly. When dry, paint them to use at your special holiday dinners. By braiding two narrow, rounded strips together, you can also make candy canes. Paint them when they are dry, and use them for holiday ornaments or tree decorations.

28. At the end of the month, write out the New Year's resolutions you would like to keep during the coming year. Check this paper in a few months to see how you are doing.

12 Construction Activities

1. Make a miniature house or building using toothpicks held together with glue. You can also use small twigs to make a log house.

2. Ask your parents if you can have some small wood scraps to glue together into the shape of cars, boats, or airplanes. Paint your creations.

3. Ask your parents for some boxes, old sheets, or blankets. Make a train, stagecoach, or house. Large packing boxes make great forts for indoors or outside.

4. Make a miniature city by covering empty Jell-O, pudding, or other small boxes with paper; paint on windows or doors, and make roofs from construction paper. Cardboard tubes from toilet tissue or paper towel rolls make great towers. To complete your city, make roads from black construction paper and grass from green paper.

5. Carve a boat from a bar of Ivory soap, using a dull butter knife to whittle the front to a pointed end. Make a hole in the center of the boat for a mast, glue a piece of paper around a stick for your sail, and put the mast in the hole. Float your boat in the bathtub or sink.

6. Using several sheets of paper, fold a whole fleet of paper airplanes, and see how far they can fly. Fold the paper different ways to see which makes the best flyer. Decorate the planes with markers or crayons before you fly them. Don't forget to pick them up afterward.

7. Make a rocket out of a cardboard tube and construction paper. Decorate it with markers or crayons.

8. Make musical instruments. You can make a guitar by putting various sizes of rubber bands across the lid of a shoe box. Strum the bands and make up tunes. Fill glasses or jars with various levels of water; then tap them lightly with a spoon or stick to make different pitched sounds. See if you can play a tune on the glasses. Make a comb harmonica by folding waxed paper and wrapping the teeth of a comb in the fold. Put your lips over the fold, and hum a tune while moving the comb from side to side. Make a flute by punching holes with a pencil in a cardboard tube. Put waxed paper or cellophane food wrap over one end, and secure it with a rubber band. Hum a tune into the uncovered end, and move your fingers on and off the holes as you do so.

9. Make a parachute by tying a 12-inch-long string to each corner of a paper napkin, then tie the loose ends of the string to a cork. Toss your parachute up, and watch it glide down gracefully.

10. Make your own phones. Take two empty cans, poke a small hole in the remaining end with a can opener, insert a 10-foot-long string, and tie a knot so that the string won't pull through the hole and come out of the can. Do the same with the other can and the other end of the string, and then hold the cans so the string is tight. Talk into the open end of the can, and listen by putting your ear close to the open end so that you can hear the other person speaking.

11. With permission, make a bottle ocean. Get a bottle or jar with a secure lid, and fill it at least halfway with water. Add a few drops of blue food coloring, and fill it the rest of the way with cooking oil. Put the top on securely, shake the bottle, and watch your magical ocean.

12. Make a paper chain. Cut paper into narrow strips, make each strip into a circle, and staple or tape the ends together. Then slip another strip through the ring and fasten the ends together. Keep on going and see how long you can make your chain.

Fun Excursions

An excursion or a day away from home each week keeps children occupied and gives them something to look forward to. Transportation arrangements must be made if youngsters cannot walk or use public transit. Perhaps you can find another parent willing to drive if you offer to help pay for the excursion. Remind your children to be on their best behavior so that the trip is pleasant for the parent in charge, and try to reciprocate when you have free time. Here are some places to go:

Public library	Beaches
Swimming pools	Bowling alleys
Roller-skating rinks	Health clubs

Flower shows	Ice-skating rinks
Parks	Tennis courts
Water slides	Movie theaters
Safe wooded areas	Restaurants
Museums	Shopping centers
Playgrounds	Video arcades
Zoo	Concerts and plays

Some places will arrange tours for children. Try these:

Fast-food restaurants	Dairies
Newspapers	Fire stations
Police stations	Hospitals
Factories	Radio and TV stations
Farms	Veterinarians
School kitchens	Banks
Waterworks	Universities
Grocery stores	Doctors and dentists
Bakeries	Senior citizen centers
Sewage plants	Power stations
Private gardens	Greenhouses
Florists	Canneries
Mines	Fish hatcheries

Check the children's section of your local newspaper for other ideas, or ask teachers or librarians about special events that would be of interest to children. The day's excursion can even be a simple trip to a friend's home, but make sure to return the favor by doing things at your home too, or take that friend along when you go on a special outing.

Classes, Clubs, Sports, and Hobbies

Classes, clubs, sports, and hobbies can help children fill free time. Many schools hold noncredit classes after school hours in such subjects as foreign languages, computers, art, music, and cooking. If this isn't the case at your child's school, see if you can interest your PTA or parent club in setting up extracurricular courses for youngsters.

Investigate summer schools; they now teach far more than just reading and arithmetic. Many community centers offer a wide variety of classes just for children.

Sports programs are frequently offered through community centers or local athletic organizations that sponsor children's teams. If your children like sports, they could be involved in some kind of sport every season of the year.

There are hundreds of hobbies for children. When exploring hobby ideas, don't choose one that is too expensive or complicated for your youngster, one that uses dangerous equipment, or one that needs a great deal of adult supervision. Start out on a small scale and invest a minimum of money until you are sure your youngster will pursue that interest. Hobby shows or arts and crafts fairs are a great place to get new ideas and meet people with similar interests.

Books, Books, and More Books

Books have entertained generations of youngsters. Children have spent countless hours learning about new places, solving mysteries, gaining new skills, and enlarging their world through reading. If you use the school, church, or public libraries, you won't have to finance these ventures. If your children aren't interested in reading, you might try paying them a small amount of money for every book read. Before long, most children are so involved in reading, the money incentive is forgotten.

Friends

Playing with friends passes free time and helps children to become socially well-adjusted; but if your children are home alone, you will have to decide whether to allow their friends to play at your place when you are not there to supervise. Parents seem to be split evenly on this decision: Half allow their children to have friends over unsupervised, and half do not. Some families allow only certain friends in the house, depending on the trustworthiness of the friend and the interaction that occurs when adults are absent. Most children think this policy is fair and seem to understand that some of their friends are more responsible than others.

It's a good idea to make your children's friends aware of your house rules and tell them that visits will continue only as long as the rules are respected. Also tell your own youngster what to do if a situation ever gets out of hand when friends are visiting. First, your child should tell the friend to go home. If that doesn't work, he should phone you at work or get help from a neighbor, and if the situation becomes very severe, he should phone the police.

Finding Friends

Although all children occasionally feel friendless, youngsters who spend time alone tend to have more problems with isolation and loneliness. If your children complain that they don't have any friends, here are some suggestions that may help them.

1. Encourage them to go to school a bit early so that they will have time to visit with classmates before school begins, but be sure that they arrive only after personnel are ready to supervise.

2. Tell your kids to fight any urge to keep to themselves. Suggest they sit with others at lunch, play with others at recess, and walk to and from school with a group. Encourage them to smile when other kids are near. Teach them to not look away or down at their feet or hide their head in a book. A smile invites further contact that might be the start of a friendship.

3. Tell your children to concentrate on other people and show an interest in their lives. When we concentrate on putting another person at ease, we tend to forget about ourselves and our own embarrassment.

4. Encourage your youngsters to become involved in school groups, clubs, or sports. This will help them pass the time, gain a skill, and meet other youngsters with similar interests.

5. The old adage "Do unto others as you would have them do unto you" is as true today as when it was first written. Teach your children that to have a friend, they must be a friend.

6. If your children cannot find friends their own age, perhaps a grandmother or grandfather or older neighbor could help fill this gap. Older people may not be able to skip rope or shoot baskets, but many love to share their knowledge of knitting, gardening, carpentry, and the like.

7. Share some of your own childhood experiences of how you found friends and dealt with boredom and loneliness. Remind your children that even the most popular and well-liked people also have times when they feel rejected and lonely.

Television and How It Affects Children

Would you allow an intruder in your home who was often violent and seemed to approve of murder, drugs, alcohol, illicit sex, and criminal behavior? Would you encourage this intruder to spend long hours in close contact with your impressionable youngsters, show them the seamy side of life, and teach them that it's normal and acceptable? Would you allow this intruder a central position in one or more rooms of your home, invite him to dinner and let him organize your family's time, schedules, and bedtime routine? This intruder is in your home right now. It's your television. Think about it!

There is no doubt that watching television is the most common way children, especially those who are home alone, spend most of their free time. In fact, the average child watches over twenty-five hours of television a week, but spends only twenty or less hours in actual classroom learning! While television does have the capacity to entertain, inform, and keep kids occupied, it's important that parents know of the medium's negative effects. Before you encourage your youngsters to watch TV during the time they are home alone, be aware of the problems of excessive TV and weigh the eventual costs.

Reading Ability

The more television a child watches, the less likely he or she is to read, and this will result in lower reading ability. The child who does not learn to read well faces lifelong difficulty, since it is estimated that 90 percent of a person's work depends on his or her ability to read. Elementary teachers report that today's children do not speak, read, understand, listen, or write as well as children did even fifteen years ago, when television was not as popular.

Creativity

Television takes up time children once spent in creative and imaginative games, make-believe, and day dreaming, all of which build emotional and creative health. When creative skills are not fostered, they do not develop.

Insensitivity to Violence

By the age of 10, children have watched an average of 400 hours of televised violence or more. By the age of 14, they have watched the killing of over 13,000 human beings! It is a proven fact that TV violence makes children less sensitive to pain and suffering in the real world, more harmfully aggressive in their behavior, and more likely to choose violence as an acceptable means to settle conflict.

Fears

Children who watch a great deal of unsupervised television are often more fearful. Monsters, werewolves, murder, robbery, rape, creatures from outer space—all common television subjects—can terrify youngsters. Since children home alone already experience fear, scary things on TV only make this problem worse.

Kiddy Consumers

Television turns children into consumers. By the time the average child is 18, he or she has watched approximately 350,000 television commercials; 55 percent of those commercials influence him to buy food, most of which is heavily sugared and low in nutrition. One study concluded that television commercials actually promote obesity in children by encouraging their consumption of high-calorie junk foods.

Commercials also influence children to want advertised toys, which appear to be big, fast, and exciting but are often disappointingly slow and small when purchased. Children do not realize that reality is often overlooked in the economic necessity to sell, sell, sell!

Social and Family Relationships

Children who are heavy television viewers are apt to be those who are already insecure and poorly adjusted socially. They cannot gain the skills needed to make friends and get along with peers if television is their main occupation. Family interaction and relationships also suffer when television is the main family activity. Some children actually seem more familiar with television characters than with their own families. They begin to expect real-life family problems to be resolved as easily and quickly (within a half-hour episode) as television family problems.

Too Much, Too Soon

Unsupervised child viewers who are exposed to adult subjects such as sex at too young an age may form distorted views of these subjects. The problem is even greater when children watch cable channels that air restricted or X-rated movies. Although there are special devices that can lock out these channels, they are used infrequently.

Psychologists are also extremely concerned about the messages MTV (Music Television, a rock video cable channel) aims at our impressionable children. They consider MTV more harmful than regular television programming because it seems to advocate drug use, violence and torture in sexual relations, and the degradation and abuse of women and children. These activities, presented by youthful rock-star models, make such behavior seem acceptable and normal. Since children have not yet developed an ability to discriminate and lack experience in most of these areas, they may form attitudes that are downright dangerous.

Stress

When television takes up the majority of a youngster's time, other healthier activities take a back seat. Children have less time for sports or active play, both of which help to release stress and tension. Excessive television viewing actually increases a child's level of stress and produces a vague feeling of emptiness.

Changing TV Habits

Since many schools are teaching youngsters about the negative influences of television and the importance of curbing excessive viewing, your children may already be aware of television's negative effects. As a first step, ask if they have noticed these effects in their own lives, or in the lives of their peers. Try to involve your entire family in this discussion, but if adults balk, at least make sure your children participate.

After talking about television's influences, try to estimate how many hours a day each child watches television. Record the estimates, then propose keeping a diary to find out how close the estimate comes to reality. Put a notebook and pencil on top of the television set and ask each child to write down the shows he or she watched and how long they lasted. At the end of a week, total up actual viewing time. Once you get a realistic look at TV viewing habits, you can decide whether or not they need changing.

If you think your children's TV habits need revision, but both you and your spouse work and thus neither of you is able to personally supervise these habits, do not despair. Many working parents who felt they could do nothing to change their children's TV habits, short of unplugging the set and carting it away every morning, have found the following suggestions helpful and far more convenient!

1. Limit television viewing. Make it a policy that the TV will not be turned on out of habit, but will only be turned on for particular programs. Have your children use a television guide to select programs they think are worthwhile, and then have them watch only those.

2. Evaluate programs. Try to watch a show with your youngsters, and afterward discuss the show and whether or not it was worthwhile. Ask the kids if they learned something or wish they had done something else that was more fun.

3. Move the television set. Put your television set where it is less accessible. Sets located away from main living areas, in unheated, uninviting, or inconvenient rooms are watched less frequently. Do *not* allow your children to have a television in their bedrooms. When children have to make a special effort to watch television, they are more apt to turn to other pursuits.

4. Rule out television at certain times. Make a rule that your family will not watch television at certain times unless there is a special exception. Before breakfast, during family mealtime, or after 9 P.M. are sensible times to rule out television for children.

5. Try other activities before turning on the TV. Make it a rule that your youngsters must make a real effort to get involved in other activities before they give up and turn on the television. Some parents even pay their children to stay involved in other more beneficial activities and forgo television.

6. Reward reduced viewing. If children limit their television viewing to a specified number of hours, offer them some sort of reward such as dinner out, a favorite meal at home, a movie, a play, or anything else that's feasible. If you are away from home unable to monitor this reduction, put your children on their honor. Some parents report they phone home and listen for background TV noise; others, who can spot a lie, ask their children directly.

7. Provide other activities. Children are less likely to watch TV when they have fun activities and things to do. The suggested activities listed earlier in this chapter give plenty of ideas for filling your children's unsupervised time.

Devices That Limit TV

There are locking devices available that permit the TV to be turned on only with a key. Households with cable TV can get a

unit that scrambles out unwanted pay channels, and it is sometimes possible to have a regular channel "detuned" and replaced
by another channel so that the undesirable channel (such as
MTV) cannot be received. If you feel these drastic measures may
be in order for your family, contact your local TV or electronics
dealer for more information.

Become a Television-Free Family

Families who have lived a television-free life (either because of
inaccessibility to TV signals or as participants in TV-free exper-
iments) report many positive effects. All families reported that
while they did sometimes miss television, the overall absence was
a positive experience. Almost all families noticed an improve-
ment in children's grades, and all reported their family relationships were strengthened by the extra time spent together playing
games, conversing, reading to one another, and working together
on projects. All families reported accomplishing more tasks and
activities without the lure of TV. They felt their youngsters exhibited more creativity—putting on plays, making up stories, and
just playing.

Most of the families who gave up television for experimental
purposes eventually returned to television; but they reported
their TV habits had changed. They were more discriminating in
their program selection and careful to monitor the effects that
television had on their family.

In Conclusion

In order to help make staying home alone a safe, successful, and
fulfilling venture for children, parents must make an effort to
ensure that the youngsters will be busy. Structured pastimes such
as after-school classes, sports, and clubs can keep youngsters occupied, while at home kids can try the hundreds of activities suggested in this chapter. By providing entertaining and engrossing
things for them to do, and limiting television viewing, parents
can help their youngsters pass free time in healthy, happy, and
beneficial activities.

Chapter 10

SAFETY AWAY FROM HOME

It's 3 o'clock and school's just out. It usually takes your child twenty minutes to walk home, but have you ever thought about your child not arriving home safe and sound?

It's 7 in the evening and your 10-year-old is at soccer practice. Will he be safe coming home on the subway? Will he be safe walking home in the dark?

It's 8 a.m. Saturday morning and your daughter is finishing up her paper route. Will she be home any minute now, ready to join the rest of the family for a day of fun?

We just assume our children will come home safe and sound, and most of the time they do. But we know that terrible, unspeakable things do happen to kids every day in cities, suburbs, and small towns. While we don't want to be constantly fearful, we also can't assume that our offspring are immune to harm. We must train our children to evaluate situations realistically and make choices that keep them safe and sound.

Keeping Children Safe in an Unsafe World

We all know that the crime rate is up and rapidly climbing and that crime and the fear of becoming its victim have changed the way we live. Doors that used to stand unlocked at night are now securely bolted. Places once frequented are now visited only at certain hours, and even then with caution. And our attitude of open trust has been replaced by one of guarded caution.

This increase in crime is also changing the way we raise our children. We are no longer able to let them go where they want, when they want, and with whom they want. We now have to temper teaching children to respect adults and to be kind and helpful with lessons on caution and knowledge of safety. We have to emphasize that a child's safety comes first.

Personal safety is not a subject parents can bring up one time and then drop. It's a subject we must incorporate into every area of our children's lives, at every stage of their personal development. When they are toddlers, we must teach them to hold our hand. When they go off to school, we teach them how to cross the street safely. When they are teenagers with more mobility and independence, we must teach them how to deal with their complicated safety needs. At every stage of growth, our children need increased safety training.

When teaching children about safety, it's important to emphasize the positive aspects, such as a greater awareness, an ability to evaluate situations and act effectively, and an increased sense of competence and confidence. We don't need to dwell on the dangers in our world or relate all the grisly horrors that can happen to children. Kids know most of these stories already from television, newspapers, and their peers. A parent's teaching goal should be caution and competence, not fearful immobilization.

Telling your youngsters how special, precious, and irreplaceable they are is the first step in safety training. Youngsters who know they are valuable are more likely to take good care of themselves, since it's a common human response to treat what is precious with care and concern. Children who have a positive self-image will usually have greater concern for their own safety than children with low self-esteem. Try some of these positive-self-image builders, coupled with a hug, loving pat, or kiss to help your child feel valued:

"You're a neat kid. We're lucky to have you."

"Have you ever stopped to realize how precious you are to me?"

"There may be other kids with your same name, but there will never be another_____ (child's name) exactly like you."

"God made you very special, precious, and unique. You are a precious gift to us."

"You know, you're one super-duper neat kid. You're not perfect, but we wouldn't trade you for anyone else in the whole wide world."

"Take good care of yourself, _____ (child's name), because I don't know what I would do without you."

"You add so much joy to my life. I had no idea any _____ year-old could be so neat."

Some parental teachings, such as telling children to obey all adults without question and to always be kind and helpful, have made kids more vulnerable and therefore more apt to get into trouble. These teachings were aimed at raising polite, caring, co-operative children—all admirable qualities. But make sure your children know that their personal safety is more important than being kind, helpful, and obedient. Assure your children that you will never be mad at them if they offend an adult, refuse a request, or appear to be rude in the process of keeping themselves safe.

When we teach children it is not safe to trust everyone, will they begin to think they cannot trust anyone? Will they think that all people are criminals? Not necessarily. You can balance this concern with positive reassurances and statements such as these:

"Most people are good and kind, but a few are not."

"If we don't know the person, we can't tell whether he is good or bad."

"These bad things will probably never happen to you, but I want you to know what to do, just in case. It's like when we put a life jacket on you in the boat. It doesn't mean we know you will fall overboard; the life jacket is your extra protection—just in case."

Teaching children personal safety does not have to make them afraid. Donald S. Smith, a family therapist with the Lutheran Counseling Network in Seattle, Washington, spoke about this concern and gave the following analogy:

> When a toddler touches a hot stove burner, he gets a painful lesson. For a long time afterward he goes out of his way to avoid getting close to the stove, but soon he becomes accustomed to its presence and learns that he won't get burned unless he actually touches a hot burner. The stove, and knowledge of it, become a part of his day-to-day life and no longer concern him, although he does clearly remember what he learned. It's the same when children first learn about personal safety. Some of the information is scary, and childish imaginations may be active. Fear and caution do start out together, but remember, the fear will rapidly vanish while the caution and knowledge remain to keep the child far safer than before.

Basic Information All Children Should Know and Have

Before your youngsters are allowed to go off alone, make sure they know the following information. Don't just assume they know it; make *sure* they do.

Your Address

Make sure your children know your street address and apartment number, if any, not just your mailing address. While speaking to thousands of school children about personal safety, I was amazed to discover that at least 10 percent of the youngsters in grades 3 through 6 did not know their street address. Unbelievable? I thought so too until I did some further checking. Some kids had recently moved and hadn't yet memorized their addresses. Some had a mailing address different from their street address. Others had simply never bothered to memorize the address. But the vast majority were children who shuttled back and forth between divorced parents and were uncertain of either address.

Emergency Phone Numbers

Does your child know the emergency phone numbers for the police department, fire department, ambulance, or medics? In many areas, 911 connects the caller with all three services; but other cities still use separate seven-digit numbers for each service. These numbers should be memorized and also prominently displayed near all phones in your home. There is a form for emergency phone numbers on page 207.

Parents' Names

Does your child know your full name, or are you simply "Dad" or "Mom"? Sometimes kids know parents' nicknames, yet more formal names are listed in telephone directories or used at work.

Important Phone Numbers

Have your children memorized your work phone number? Do they know a nearby neighbor's phone number? Even if you have the type of phone that can be programmed to automatically dial certain numbers by pressing one digit, be certain your children have memorized important phone numbers. Do not let them rely solely on technology, because they may be away from that machine when they need to phone you.

Also show them how to use a pay phone, and explain that on most pay phones, you can dial the operator or emergency numbers without depositing money. If the child needs to make a call and has no money, it is usually possible to call the operator and reverse the charges (call collect) from a pay phone.

Identification Card

Make sure your children carry some sort of an identification card in their backpack, book bag, pocket, or purse. It is also a good idea for them to carry a second card or have an instant replacement at home in case they lose the first one. There is a sample card in the Appendix. Any ID card should list medical information that could prove invaluable to medical or hospital staff in case of an accident. The card should also have a list of phone numbers of people to be contacted in case of emergency. All of this information can be written on a 3 x 5 index card. It's also a good idea to securely tape a few quarters to the back of the ID card so your child will always have spare money.

Basic Safety Rules for Children

These basic safety rules will help keep your children safe and sound. Be sure to explain the why of the rules because children are much more likely to follow rules when they understand the reasons behind them.

Go Directly Home and Use the Same Route Every Day

Make sure your children know they should take the same route each time when they are returning from school, a friend's house, or other activities. When children use a different route, take a detour, or go somewhere else without telling us, we can't know where to find them for something as mundane as a dentist appointment or as alarming as an emergency. Most parents also know how long it normally takes a child to reach home and worry when the child is later than usual. If your children want to use a different route, or not come straight home, make it a rule that they must ask your permission in advance.

When children use the same route daily, they also become familiar with any potential dangers along that route, and where they can get help if need be. They learn which houses are usually occupied at that time of day, where friends live, which businesses are friendly to kids, the location of pay phones, and public establishments along the way. They also become familiar with safe homes or businesses. These places can be identified by a special sticker or sign displayed in their window indicating they have agreed to be havens for children who need help or are in danger (see also page 189).

There's Safety in Numbers

Encourage your youngster to stay with a group rather than travel alone. There is safety in numbers, and it's usually more fun to be in a group. If children must walk alone, have them carry a whistle or other device to attract attention if they need help.

Look Alive!

It has been proven that the way children carry themselves has an effect on their personal safety. The child who is daydreaming and shambling along in an uncertain way is much more likely to be bothered than the youngster who looks self-assured, alert, and in control. Even when lost or confused, youngsters should try to give the impression they know where they are going.

Avoid Dangerous Places

Teach your children to avoid the following dangerous areas, never to play there, and never to take a shortcut through them:

Wooded areas	Vacant lots
Deserted areas	Abandoned buildings
Teenage hangouts	Taverns or bars
Construction sites	
Streams, lakes, swamps	Neighborhoods known to be dangerous
Railroad tracks	
Furnace rooms or storage areas in apartment buildings	Fields of livestock
	Garbage dumps or car dumps

It's a good idea for parents to walk the routes their children use and point out any potentially dangerous areas or conditions. At the same time, indicate places such as homes of friends or public places like stores, gas stations, and restaurants where children might get help if necessary. Also point out homes or businesses that have agreed to be havens for children in trouble. See page 189 for more information on these safety programs.

Here's how one family dealt with a dangerous place in their neighborhood. An apartment building being built nearby was attracting kids like a magnet. Parents worried about the youngsters being around the construction and heavy equipment and finally found an effective way to keep the kids safe yet not restrict them completely from the site.

They talked to the construction foreman about the problem and found that he, too, was concerned about the children getting in the way or getting hurt. He suggested roping off a special viewing area, where the young sidewalk superintendents could safely watch the action yet not be in the way. Not only was this compromise good for community relations between the builder and the neighbors; it also kept the kids safe. If you don't have the good fortune to work with such an agreeable foreman, it's best to forbid your kids to visit a construction site unless you are with them.

Staying Safe After Dark

If your children must be out after dark, encourage them to stay with a group or at least one other person, travel on well-lighted streets, and avoid dark or deserted areas. A shortcut just might turn out to be the long way home if they run into trouble.

Make sure children out at night wear light-colored clothes or have reflective tape on their clothing. This tape can be purchased at fabric stores and can be sewn on outer wear such as jackets, pants, or hats. It can also be glued onto backpacks, book bags, shoes, or boots. Police departments in many cities give out reflective badges to attach to children's clothing.

Children do not appreciate how hard it is for drivers to see at night, especially if the weather is bad. They seem to believe if they can see an oncoming car, the driver can see them just as well. The next time you drive your children somewhere at night, use that opportunity to point out how difficult it is to see someone in dark clothing walking alongside a road. Show them how much easier it is to spot someone in the car headlights when the person is dressed in light-colored clothing and walking facing the oncoming traffic.

Hitchhiking Is Life-Threatening

Children have repeatedly been told about the dangers of accepting rides with strangers, yet kids still hitchhike, and, unfortunately, many of them end up injured or even murdered. Make sure your children understand they are not to hitchhike *under any circumstance*. Suggest alternatives in case they find themselves stranded, provide a list of people who can be called for a ride in an emergency, and keep a taxi fund at home in case they need to call a cab. Be sure to set a good example yourself by never hitchhiking or picking up a hitchhiker.

Crossing Streets

Kids have been told to be careful crossing streets ever since they were old enough to walk, but often this caution is not heeded. Over 5 percent of children in one survey reported they, or a family member, had been involved in a traffic accident while they were walking. With this figure in mind, review these traffic rules with your children.

1. Children should always look both ways before crossing the street and allow plenty of time so that they don't have to run. If they are not sure they have ample time to cross, they should wait.

2. Pedestrians should cross streets only at corners and look all four ways in case cars are turning.

3. Pedestrians should not jaywalk (cross in the middle of the block) or walk out between parked cars.

4. Pedestrians should cross with the green light or walk sign. But don't assume that these will give them complete protection, because some drivers will run a red light or speed up to make it through an intersection on the yellow caution light. Drivers may also be turning and expect pedestrians to get out of their way.

5. Pedestrians should be cautious of cars every day, but be especially careful on rainy or foggy days when drivers cannot see well and roads may be slippery. When streets are icy, children should keep well back from the road and watch for cars that may skid on the slick surface.

6. If there are sidewalks on their route, your youngsters should use them. They should walk in the center of the sidewalk away from dark doorways, hedges, or trees. If they must walk along the edge of the street or road, remind them to walk *facing* oncoming traffic and be alert for cars being driven erratically.

7. Children should obey all police officers and safety officers, including school crossing guards; they are there for the youngsters' protection and safety.

When reviewing traffic safety rules, it is important for parents to emphasize again that not all drivers are law-abiding. In some urban areas, it is estimated there is only a 50:50 chance that drivers will stop for a red light. Drivers everywhere are ignoring speed limits. All too often, school crossing signs are ignored. It is certainly no secret that we still have drunk drivers on our roads in spite of improved state laws and organizations such as Mothers Against Drunk Drivers (MADD) or Students Against Drunk Drivers (SADD).

Special Safety Situations

There are some situations which present special safety problems to youngsters. It is important to discuss the following situations with your children and practice the correct action you want them to take.

Buckle Up!

Studies indicate that each year one out of every five Americans is involved in a motor vehicle collision. Car accidents continue to be the leading cause of death or injury to children and adolescents. Seat belts not only prevent car occupants from being thrown out of a vehicle, but save them from being thrown around inside as well. Even at speeds as low as 3 to 6 miles an hour, children may be injured during sudden stops or turns.

Seat belts so effectively lower auto injury and death rates that many states have made it a law that seat belts or child restraint devices must be used by all occupants of private vehicles. Whether or not your state has a seat belt law, insist and keep insisting that your children buckle up, not only in your car but also when they ride with others. Make it a family rule that the car does not start until the driver and all riders are buckled up. When kids get into the habit of wearing a seat belt in the family car, they will be more likely to buckle up in any car, at any age. This good habit, formed early, will do the most to offer your children protection in a vehicle. Don't let your children risk a tragedy like Lynnette's.

Lynnette's mother was driving her to a nearby gymnastic lesson when another driver went through a stop sign and collided with them. It seemed a minor crash; both cars were traveling under the 25-miles-an-hour speed limit. However, Lynnette was not wearing a seat belt; she was thrown violently around inside the car and hit her head against the door handle. She remained in a coma for two weeks, and when she regained consciousness, it was determined that she was paralyzed from the waist down. There would be no further dream of a gymnast in that family.

Carpooling

In order to keep children safe and parents sane, rules are usually necessary when children ride in a car pool. Here are some suggestions.

- Everyone must be buckled into a seat belt.
- There will be no roughhousing.
- Hands, arms, and feet must be kept inside the car (not out the windows).
- Nothing is to be thrown from the car.
- Noise must be kept at acceptable limits, to be determined by the driver.

Do Not Ride with a Drunk, Ever!

Tell your children they must *never* ride with a driver they suspect has been drinking, is drinking, or is drunk. Give your kids other ideas of how to get where they're going, such as calling a taxi, walking if the distance isn't too great, riding with someone else, or calling home or a neighbor for a ride. Since this situation calls for a great deal of assertiveness, it helps if you practice it in advance with your children. If they have role-played this drama beforehand, children will be better able to handle it in real life. (When you role-play the part of the drunk driver, make sure there is no humor, since such a situation is not a laughing matter—it's dead serious.)

If Your Child's Ride Does Not Come

Sometimes drivers who are to pick up children are delayed or don't show up because of an emergency, forgetfulness, or other reasons. This can be upsetting for a child who doesn't know what has happened or what to do. Give your children some suggestions ahead of time in case this situation arises. Possible suggestions are (1) use the phone at school or ask to use the phone in a store or other public place, (2) walk if the route is not dangerous or the distance too great, or (3) call a taxi. Many families have set aside money at home that could be used to pay taxi fare. The identification card on page 203 would be helpful to a stranded child, since it lists phone numbers the child could call and has money (if taped on as suggested earlier) for a pay phone.

Riding the School Bus

Although most school-bus drivers make their young riders aware of the rules, it's a good idea for parents to reinforce these safety suggestions.

1. Kids need to allow plenty of time to get to a bus stop so that they won't have to run for the bus.

2. When waiting for a bus, youngsters should stand at the edge of the road, but not on it; they should also keep a sharp watch for traffic. Remind your children that if they cross the street to board the bus, they must look both ways before stepping out. Traffic is supposed to stop for the flashing warning lights displayed by a school bus, but not all drivers are careful and law-abiding.

3. Remind your children not to push, shove, or crowd when they get on a bus. One at a time up the stairs and down the aisles is best.

4. Riders should sit down as soon as possible and keep the main aisle clear of book bags, musical instruments, and lunch sacks.

5. Kids must stay seated and not move around when the bus is underway. They should not get up until the bus has come to a complete stop.

6. Students should never stick arms, hands, or feet out the windows or throw anything from the bus.

7. If your youngsters have problems with other children on the bus, instruct them to tell the bus driver or their teacher.

Assaults and drug problems, including using and dealing drugs, are serious problems on some school buses. If your child ever mentions these, meet with school officials and suggest having a parent or teacher attendant ride the bus until these problems are taken care of.

Public Transit

If your children ride public transit, go over these safety tips.

1. Children should know where they are going and where to get off before boarding the bus or subway.

2. Encourage your child to sit near the driver or conductor if possible. Conductors can answer questions or look out for the youngster if trouble occurs, but caution your child not to bother them unnecessarily.

3. Children who flash money around are just inviting someone to steal it. Parents should investigate ways of purchasing subway or bus tickets ahead of time so that children do not have to carry cash for the fare. If your children must pay the fare in cash, tell them to keep their money out of sight in a purse, pocket, book bag, or backpack, which they keep with them at all times. Whether they use tickets or cash, make sure your youngsters have enough money for a second fare in case they get lost and have to pay a second fare.

4. Make sure your children know they are not to block exits or aisles.

5. Encourage your children to be considerate of others—no food, drink, noisy radios, or tape players. Usually no pets, except guide dogs for the blind, are allowed on public transit.

6. Tell your kids to keep alert and not daydream or sleep when riding public transit because they could miss their stop or be unaware of problems developing around them.

Safety at School

Even though your school administration tries very hard to keep children safe while they are in school, this concern must be shared by the home as well. Here are some school safety tips parents should teach their children.

1. To help keep your youngsters from suffering a robbery or assault, warn them never to take anything to school that is irreplaceable or of great value. If they wear rings, they should not remove them while washing hands or showering after gym.

2. School lockers are not as secure as they seem to be. Caution your children not to tell other kids their locker combination and to make sure it has been changed from the previous year.

3. Make sure your children have a secure pocket or purse in which to carry lunch money. Better yet, consider having them buy a lunch ticket. At most schools, the ticket is kept by the lunchroom personnel, so it is not apt to be lost or stolen. If your children buy a lunch ticket, write a check so that they don't have to carry that much cash.

4. Caution your students to be very careful not to leave possessions when they change classes or leave for the day. A new jacket left in homeroom will very likely be gone when the child comes back to retrieve it.

5. Warn your children to be cautious if a group of students is quieter or noisier than normal or if the group seems to be crowding around something. This may mean trouble.

6. If your children observe others fighting at school, they should get help from an adult rather than try to break it up themselves.

7. Bathrooms at some schools can be dangerous places even during the school day. If a student seems to be standing guard at the bathroom door, something out of the ordinary may be going on. Caution your child not to go in under such circumstances, but to seek help from an adult.

8. If your children are ever threatened, robbed, or assaulted at school, encourage them to tell you or another trusted adult as soon as possible, even if they were threatened with further violence if they report the incident. Law enforcement officials say that reprisals are not commonplace if the situation is reported and promptly dealt with by school authorities.

9. Parents should make sure youngsters do not arrive at school before personnel are ready to supervise or stay at school after teachers have gone home in the afternoon. Children who do stay for scheduled after-school activities should be told to be very cautious in the deserted school building and not to wander down dimly lit halls. If they see a person in the building who does not seem to belong, they should leave that area immediately and notify an adult in charge. Remind your youngsters to take a friend along when using the bathroom or locker room after regular school hours.

10. Depending on your school, it may be wise to have your kids avoid the buildings or school grounds during evenings, weekends, and school vacations.

Constant discrimination or harassment can often be serious enough for parents to consider transferring a child to another school. If this situation occurs, discuss it with school administrators to see what can be done. If you do not feel your local school officials have paid enough attention to your particular problem, contact the superintendent of schools. If that does not produce the desired effect, bring your problem before the school board.

Dealing with a Mean Dog

Almost everyone, adult or child, will sometime have to deal with a threatening dog. Here is what professional animal control officers and guard dog trainers recommend you tell your children.

1. If a dog threatens you, do not run. Do not point a finger or wave your arms at the dog, since these actions may only provoke it into biting. The best action is to stand perfectly still with your hands clasped in front of you. Usually the animal will sniff you, lose interest, and go away.

2. If the animal does not leave, say "No!" or "Bad dog!" in a loud voice. He won't know how frightened you are if you make your voice sound very angry. When you appear angry, a dog believes you are in control of the situation and is more apt to mind you and retreat.

3. Do not turn your back on a menacing animal. If you appear angry and not afraid, it is unlikely a dog will attack. If the dog seems to be losing interest in you, try walking slowly and carefully backward, still saying "No!" and "Bad dog!" Glance around for adults who could help you if the situation worsens. If the dog advances, stand still again.

4. In the rare case that a dog actually attacks, try to stay on your feet. Deflect its attacks with your shoulder or hip and continue to shout angrily at him "No!" or "Bad Dog!" Be very careful about trying to hit or kick an attacking dog because such action may provoke it even more. You may also lose your balance and fall, and you don't have much protection from an animal when you are on the ground. If the animal is very small and you think you can kick it safely, do so. This may sound cruel, but it is threatening to hurt you.

5. If an animal runs at you while you are riding your bike, try to keep your balance and stop. Slowly get off the bike, keeping it between you and the animal, then angrily tell it "No!" Never try to outrun a dog. If you know there is a dog that may cause trouble on your bike route, get off your bike and walk it past that area.

6. Never tease an animal that is confined to a yard or chained. If it should get loose or break its chain, you could be held responsible for provoking an attack.

7. Be sure to report any dog attack to your local animal control agency, police department, and the dog's owner so that action can be taken to keep the animal from threatening others.

8. If you are actually bitten, get medical help first (see page 78 for first aid for animal bites), then report the incident to the animal control agency or police department. The offending animal must be observed for a period of days to make sure it does not have rabies. Although the newer rabies shots are far less painful than they used to be, you still don't want to have to undergo them needlessly.

9. If you come upon any animal that has been injured or hit by a car, do not touch it. Leave it and get help immediately. Even a loving pet may bite if it is hurt or confused.

10. Never handle dead animals. If they had rabies, the disease can be passed to you through small scratches, hangnails, or even tiny nicks on your hands.

Many cities have recently adopted special ordinances concerning breeds of dogs whose attacks are especially dangerous and severe, such as pit bull terriers. If such breeds or other dogs known to be dangerous run loose in your neighborhood, talk to the owners about making sure the animals are always penned or on a leash. If the owner is uncooperative, you may need to take aggressive action by contacting your local animal control or police department and insisting that the animal be confined or impounded.

Safety in Elevators

Elevators can be dangerous spots for anyone alone, since a large number of assaults, muggings, and other crimes take place there. Children should be told that if they ever feel the least bit uncomfortable about riding with a person who is also waiting for the elevator, they should use an excuse such as, "Oops, I forgot to pick up the mail," or "Oh dear, I forgot something," or "I better wait for my dad." Then they should turn and leave, get help, or wait for the next elevator car.

They can use similar excuses if the elevator comes and they feel uncomfortable about riding with the person already in it. If children are in an elevator alone and someone gets on who makes them feel uneasy, they should get off at the first opportunity. Children should be told that they do not always have to provide a stranger with an excuse.

Show your children that elevator control panels are equipped with an alarm button to summon help, and advise them that it is a good idea if they try to stand near that control panel when riding in an elevator. Be very sure your youngsters know they must never play in elevators or push the alarm button in fun.

If Your Child Is Lost

At some time during childhood, most kids get separated from those they are with and become lost! This situation can cause nightmares for both parents and children. It is bad enough for youngsters to have this experience close to home or at least in their own general neighborhood, but it can be much worse when they are strangers in a large city. Before your children have to face the frightening situation of being lost, teach them what to do and how to get help. When youngsters have this basic knowledge, they are better able to handle the situation safely.

Be especially watchful when you take children to an unfamiliar place or to a place where there are crowds of people, such as large stores, shopping centers, bus stations, airport terminals, theaters, fairs, or carnivals.

1. Tell your children they must not panic if they discover they are lost; they should try to calm down and remember the things you have taught them.

2. Caution your youngsters to be very careful whom they ask for help. Their first choice should be a police officer, fire fighter, medic, or a store security guard. Store clerks or personnel are also good choices, as are people in positions of authority, such as lifeguards or park rangers.

3. Although you have taught your children not to talk to strangers, tell them there may come a time when they won't be able to find the choices listed above and will have to ask a stranger for help. If this happens, their safest choice is a nicely dressed man and woman with children (a family). Other safe choices would be a nicely dressed woman with children, a middle-aged woman, or a grandmotherly looking woman. A nicely dressed couple would be another choice. This advice may seem sexist, but it is quite reliable. Women have proven to be more compassionate and willing to help children, and it is an unfortunate reality that the majority of people who prey upon youngsters are men.

4. Make sure your youngsters understand that if they are lost in a store or shopping center, it is very important that they stay inside the building and not wander around the parking lot looking lost and alone—an easy target for abduction.

Lost in the Woods

If your family spends a good deal of time outdoors, you may have already made sure your children know basic rules of the trail and outdoor survival. It is also important to teach them what to do if they should ever become lost in the woods.

1. Again, the first rule is not to panic. Instead children should sit down and calm down. While resting, they should try to think back to where they became lost. It may be just a few steps back to where they accidentally stepped off the path or took the wrong turn. Clear thinking and calm actions often help hikers find the way back quickly.

2. If they can't find the way back to a familiar point within ten or fifteen minutes, children should not use up valuable energy or risk getting lost even further. They should stay put and wait to be found. If they are on a path, they should stay there, since rescuers usually walk the paths first when searching.

3. Kids should make themselves as obvious as possible while waiting to be found. A whistle is invaluable because its sound carries further than the human voice. The recognized distress signal is three blasts on a whistle, then a pause to listen, then three more blasts and a pause, and so on. If there is a nearby clearing and youngsters can spare a brightly colored piece of clothing, it should be laid out so it can be seen from a high spot or by search planes.

4. If they are lost, children should stay quiet and conserve their energy, keeping as warm as possible. Generally, even skinny little kids can live without food for at least a week if they have water, so they should not expend precious energy looking for food. If they are cold or it is raining, a fallen log will provide some shelter or a cover of leaves or even dirt may help them to stay warm.

5. Although kids seem to worry about wild animals attacking them, forest creatures are generally not a great threat. Avoid all animal mothers with young if possible, but remember that most wild animals are afraid of humans and will retreat if given the chance.

Children and Bikes

Remember when you rode your very first two-wheeler? That unsteady ride was not only the beginning of many years of biking fun, but also the start of a very dangerous time. Accidents involving bikes and cars are one of the leading causes of death and serious injury to children. Most often it is the young cyclist who is at fault. So when we help our youngsters take their very first bike ride, we must teach them to do it safely.

The first step to safe biking is to ride a safe bike. Usually the parents are responsible for bike maintenance until children are able to take care of it themselves. Here are some suggestions for keeping your child's bike in good shape.

1. Keep tires inflated to the proper pressure especially if a bike has been unused for any length of time. Usually the pressure limit is shown on the side of the tire and can be checked with a tire gauge. It is also a good idea to inspect tires every so often for cracks, cuts, or bulges.

2. Make sure your child's bike has proper reflectors and headlights. Safety officials still advise against children riding bikes after dark, even with a proper headlight.

3. Storing a bike out of the weather will help keep it in good shape and inhibit rust.

4. Keep nuts and bolts tightened securely. Use the proper wrench; some bikes require a metric wrench, and others a regular one.

5. Check the brakes every so often to see if they work well, since this part of a bike often needs adjustment.

6. Keep the chain, wheel axles, and other moving parts clean and lightly oiled.

7. Make sure handle grips are securely attached to handlebars.

8. Purchase a children's bike helmet and encourage its regular use to lessen the chance of head injury if your child is thrown from the bike or in an accident.

Besides making sure a bike is safe to ride, make sure the bike itself is secure. Buy a strong bike lock for your children to use and encourage them to use it every time they leave the bike. The bike should be locked to something permanent like a pole, post, or bike rack so that the whole bike can't simply be carried off. But bikes should not be left unattended for long periods of time, since most chains and locks can be easily cut if a thief has plenty of time to do so. A thief may try to take your child's bike by force. Emphasize that a life is more important to you than a bike, and warn your child not to endanger himself in any way. A bike can be replaced, but a child cannot!

Make it a rule that bikes are to be put away at night. Bikes left out on the lawn or street are an invitation to a thief. If children ride a bike to a friend's home, urge them to park it in the backyard or lock it up, not just leave it out front and hope that it will still be there when it's time to go home.

Many hours of practice are needed from the first unsteady solo ride until the child is ready to ride in traffic. Safe biking requires good sense and a knowledge of safety rules. One way to test your child's riding skill and knowledge is to have him or her participate in a bike marathon. If your youngster's school doesn't have a bike safety day, ask your local police department to schedule one. Usually bikes can be registered at the same time. Keep this registration, a photo of the bike, and any other pertinent information to help identify the bike if it's ever lost or stolen.

Teach your kids to regard the bike as their "vehicle." The rules that apply to cars also apply to bikes when they're ridden in traffic. With this in mind, make sure your young bikers follow these traffic rules.

1. In traffic, stay to the right of the road, and always move in the *same* direction as the car traffic.

2. Obey all traffic signs and stoplights, and keep a safe distance from the vehicle in front.

3. Use proper hand signals to alert other drivers of turns and stops.

4. Ride defensively; always be aware of other drivers. Be extra cautious at intersections where turning drivers may not see you. Also, watch for road hazards such as glass, sewer grates, rocks, or car doors opening suddenly.

5. Although it's fun, don't give others a ride on the handlebars. A passenger can upset your bike's balance and block your vision. If you must carry books or packages on your bike, be sure to use a basket, rack, or backpack.

6. Don't wear long, loose clothing which can get caught in the wheel spokes or chain. Buy pant leg clips, or use a simple rubber band.

7. Use extreme caution in bad weather and don't ride if streets are slick, icy, or snow-covered.

8. It's best if you don't ride after dark. If you must ride after dark, you must wear light-colored or reflective clothing and use bike headlights and reflectors.

Although dogs love to run with their owners, parents should enforce a rule that when children go bike riding, pets must be left at home. Most cities have leash laws and kids trying to manage a bike and a leash could have a serious accident. Pets are also apt to attract other animals who might bother your biker.

Parents must take a firm stand against dangerous bicycle antics, especially in traffic. If you observe your son or daughter riding dangerously, give a very firm first warning. The next time such behavior is observed, restrict the use of the bike for a period of time. Do not be lenient about dangerous biking because the majority of bike accidents are caused not by drivers but by children who ride unsafely.

Teach your children that safe bikers are also courteous. They do not endanger other people on sidewalks or bike paths, and they do not ride on or cut across other people's property, especially lawns.

Teach Your Children to Be Prepared

Trusting an Instinctive Feeling

An "instinctive" or "intuitive" feeling is a deep, nagging, some-times uncomfortable feeling that there is danger ahead. It's like a sixth sense, trying to tell us something important about a sit-uation, and it has enabled many people to avoid or even avert personal harm. Law enforcement officials advise people to trust these feelings and act accordingly to keep themselves safe.

It's hard to explain to children what you mean when you tell them to trust their "intuition" or "instinct," but it's vital that you try. Explain that this feeling is rare and not the result of a child's overactive imagination. Some youngsters can imagine a mugger behind every bush or a burglar breaking in every time a gust of wind rattles a tree branch against the house, but this feeling is very different. Make sure your children understand that an in-stinctive feeling is usually a rare response to possible danger. You could liken it to a gut-level feeling that things are not all right. If you have ever had a personal experience with this feeling, re-late it to your children, or tell them the following stories.

Aisha and her cousin were walking home after playing at the school one evening. Aisha suddenly had a strong feeling that they should not walk the usual way home and convinced her cousin to walk down another street. When they were almost home they heard police sirens and later learned a young man on the street they avoided had shot his family and a neighbor after a bitter argument. Aisha's listening to her feelings and acting on them may have kept the youngsters out of harm's way.

Jose had just four blocks to walk from the subway station to his apartment. One evening he had a nagging feeling he was in danger, so he phoned his mother from the station, told her of his fear, and asked her to come get him. His mother refused to come. As he walked home alone, two young thugs jumped Jose, beat him up, and stole his wallet.

Tell your children if they ever have an instinctive feeling that they are in danger, being followed, or the like, they should im-mediately do whatever they have to to keep themselves safe. Let them know you will honor their feelings, back them up, and do whatever you can to help them stay safe.

Getting a Description or License Plate Number

Teach your child the importance of getting a clear description of people, cars, and vehicle license numbers in cases where something bad happens. Police can do very little without this information. When getting a car description, the most important thing to do is to get the license plate number. They can write this number down, scratch it in the dirt or on a rock, or repeat it over and over until it is memorized. Other identifying features such as the make of the car, the model, any dents, or unusual equipment, such as special lights or roll bars, can also be helpful to authorities.

Police will want to know the person's skin color, hair color, and color of eyes. They will also want to know if the person had any scars, tatoos, or other distinguishing features, such as a beard or mustache, as well as how the person was dressed. Children probably cannot estimate the person's height and weight, but they can come pretty close if they make a comparison to someone they know well, such as a father, brother, or aunt. They can gauge whether the person was taller, shorter, fatter, or thinner than Mom or Uncle Bob. Police may also ask which way the person went, what was said during a conversation, if any particular names were mentioned, or if the person had an accent.

A Stranger May Mean Danger

Between 1984 and 1987, I taught personal safety to over 10,000 children in grades 1 through 6 attending schools in various economic areas ranging from affluent to impoverished. During the introduction I asked these children if they knew they should not talk to strangers. I often got a look that said, "Oh come on, that's baby stuff," and they assured me they knew better than to talk to strangers.

Later on in my presentation I used a series of role-playing activities that were based on actual incidents where an adult had tried to lure a child. First, I told the group to imagine I was a well-dressed man driving a nice-looking car. I pretended to pull the car over next to a youngster who was walking to school. Holding a map, I asked for directions to a nearby, well-known location. A shocking 75 percent of the children who participated in this play unhesitatingly came over to my imaginary car, looked at the map, and tried to help me out. A few even offered to get in my car and show me the way! Just minutes before, these same youngsters had assured me they never talked to strangers.

Next, I took the part of a man who had a box of kittens in his car. I pretended to drive over to a group of youngsters and asked them to come look at the darling kittens I needed to give away. After being so easily tricked the first time, the children were now more hesitant to approach, but I could still lure them closer by saying I was on my way to the lake to drown the kittens because I couldn't find homes for them.

Children often think a "stranger" is ill-kempt and dangerous-looking, but that is not true. Teach your child that a "stranger" is *anyone* they do not know. It doesn't matter how a person is dressed, what he says or how safe he seems to be. A stranger may be:

- The man with a cast on his arm you've seen a few times around your apartment building but do not actually know
- The nicely dressed woman you do not know who says your mom told her to give you a ride home today
- The man who asks you to help him find his dog
- The teenage paperboy you do not know who says he needs your help delivering papers and asks you to come down to his basement to get the papers
- The man with a camera who says he's a newspaper photographer and wants to take your picture in the woods
- The couple you don't know who offer you a ride home while you're waiting at the bus stop
- The man watching your soccer game who wants to give you a new soccer ball he isn't using
- The old woman you do not know who offers you lemonade in her house.

These "strangers" may be ordinary people with legitimate requests, but children just cannot take a chance. Since it is impossible for children to judge the safety of a situation, we must teach them to follow these steps when dealing with any stranger.

1. Say no or shake your head to any requests by a stranger.

2. Next, step backward away from the stranger so that you are out of reach just in case the person tries to grab you.

3. Quickly leave by walking or running away.

4. Report the incident to a trusted adult who can follow up if he or she believes the incident was dangerous.

We have taught our youngsters to be compassionate and helpful, but this very behavior can also put them in danger. When children are away from home, it's safest if they mind their own business. No matter whether they see a fight, a mugging, a stalled car, or a person in trouble, they should stay away. The most your child should do is to go to a phone or a home to get help for the person in trouble. The information below will help your child evaluate which home or person is a safe choice.

Being Followed by a Stranger

Since it's not an uncommon experience for children to discover a stranger is following them, it is important to teach your youngsters how to handle this situation.

If a car is following a child who is on foot or on a bicycle, she can quickly turn around and walk or ride in the other direction, so the car will have to make a U turn or back up to continue following. This gives the child a few extra seconds to get away or decide where to get help.

A child can also run to a public place such as a store, gas station, restaurant, or hospital, where there will be people who can help her. Some areas have special programs such as "Block Parent," "Helping Hand," "McGruff Houses," "Safe Haven," or "Safe Home," usually administered by elementary school PTAs or local police departments. These homes or businesses can be identified by special signs displayed in a window. The people in these homes, apartments, or businesses have agreed to help youngsters who are lost, in danger, or need help. Usually the police department has checked to see if the owners are reliable and safe.

Point out these signs ahead of time to your child, and explain what they mean.

When I talk to children about these safe homes, they always ask me if bad people ever use those signs to lure unsuspecting children. I reply that I have had such a sign in my window for over ten years and during all that time, not a single child has come to my door for help. A "bad guy" using such a sign is probably in for a long wait and would quickly give up and use an easier way to lure youngsters. However, if you have reason to suspect the validity of a home or business displaying such a sign, contact the neighborhood elementary school or police department and tell them of your concern.

If someone is following your child in a residential area and there are no safe homes nearby, tell her to go to the nearest home that looks occupied, neat, and well-cared for. Although this value judgment is not always a valid one, it is usually reliable. People who keep up their homes are generally more apt to be responsible, trustworthy, and compassionate to a child needing help.

If a child is being followed close to home, she should not go there if the house is empty. Instead she should go to a neighbor and phone the police. If the first neighbor she tries is not home, she should try another until she gets help.

It is sometimes effective for a child being followed to pretend to see an adult friend or parent and call out to him, or even to go up to a home that looks occupied and call out, "Hi, Mom, I'm home," or some similar greeting. Such a ruse often discourages a pursuer.

If a Stranger Grabs Your Child

First reassure your youngsters that a stranger will probably never grab them, but you want them to know what to do, just in case. It's like a fire drill at school; all kids take part in the drill, yet very few, if any, of those children are ever involved in a school fire. Fire drills are practiced so the youngsters will know exactly what to do. Telling children what to do if someone grabs them is like the school fire drill.

1. If grabbed, a child should do everything possible to raise a fuss and attract lots of attention, then escape. Encourage your youngster to struggle, shriek, scream at the top of his lungs, blow a whistle, etc. A child's first reaction is to scream "Help!" but it's far more effective to scream "Fire!" People are so used to hearing children call for help in play that they are less likely to respond to this word. On the other hand, almost everyone will respond to the word "Fire!" since fires are exciting events that do not usually put spectators in personal danger. Screaming "Fire!" may also serve to confuse and distract an attacker. Make sure your youngster knows not to scream "Fire!" in fun, since this shock word can cause people to panic.

2. How hard should a child try to get away? Most police and safety personnel agree that a child should struggle as hard as possible (1) if the person who grabbed him does not have a gun or knife and (2) if the child's chances of attracting attention or escaping are good. Biting, scratching, kicking, and stomping on the attacker's feet are tactics a child can use. If these actions enrage the attacker, the child should cease but continue to watch for an opportunity to escape. Convicted criminals report they usually released a child who put up a good fight or made a fuss because they were afraid of attracting attention.

3. If the attacker shows a gun or knife, tell your child not to resist, since he has little chance of safely overpowering an adult with a weapon. In this situation, it is best for the child to obey the attacker and watch for an opportunity to escape. It is difficult even for an adult to cope with situations where a weapon is used. There are no specific rules that will prove effective in every situation, so tell your child to act in a way that seems safest and to avoid any heroics that could lead to his serious injury or even death.

4. Young boys (rarely girls) often think they are more than a match for any attacker, no matter how big or strong the bad guy may be. They boast about punching, throwing, or killing anyone who tries to get them and talk of using their dad's gun or mom's butcher knife. If your child thinks he can overpower an adult, and most people who grab kids are adult men, make him realize he has a very slim chance of coming out the winner in such a situation. Squelch this show of foolish bravado because it could be very dangerous.

5. Often youngsters who have had lessons in self-defense say they feel much safer than before. While such classes may give the child a feeling of self-confidence, they can be a problem if the youngster gets a false sense of security or is unrealistic about his physical limits. If your child takes self-defense classes, make sure he realizes there is no shame in fleeing rather than fighting when the odds are against him.

6. If a child is grabbed and thrown into a car, the youngster should not voluntarily fasten his seat belt but should stay near the door, ready to jump out if there is a safe opportunity to escape. The driver has to stop sometime for gas, food, to use the bathroom, or at a red light, and the child should be ready to escape or get help from a nearby adult.

7. In my classes kids usually come up with a few offbeat responses when I ask them what they would do if they were grabbed. Although these responses always evoke laughter from the group, they may prove effective in a real-life situation. One child said he would wet his pants; another replied he would "probably crap" (his very words); another said she would vomit all over. All three of these responses would make a child much less desirable to an attacker! Pretending to faint, acting mentally ill, and feigning an asthma attack or epileptic seizure are other responses that have been successfully used to thwart an attack. These unexpected actions may catch the attacker off guard, and he may leave his victim alone.

Kidnapping: The Ultimate Agony

Child abduction is something parents don't like to talk about, yet it is a concern to all of us. Each year in the United States over 1 million children are reported missing. Up to 90 percent of these youngsters have run away and eventually do return home, but many of the rest are victims of abduction—either by a parent in a divorce custody fight (an estimated 100,000 children) or by a stranger (an estimated 50,000 cases). The majority of children kidnapped by a stranger simply disappear without a clue, never to return. You can help protect your children against abduction by following these rules and explaining their importance.

1. Make sure your children memorize their home phone number, including the area code. They should also know how to make a collect call home without adult help. Children should also memorize their street address, city, and state.

2. Always know where your children are. If they go somewhere after school, tell them to phone you at work or leave you a note at home.

3. Never leave young children unattended in stores, parking lots, parks, or public areas; keep them with you. Shopping malls, carnivals, fairs, and other festivals are especially dangerous. Make sure your children know exactly what to do if they become separated from you or lost (see page 181).

4. Since public restrooms are known to be places abductors frequent, go in with your child or at least stand outside near the door so that your child can holler if there is trouble.

5. Discourage children from wearing clothing displaying their name. Kids tend to trust someone who calls them by name and are much less suspicious of a person who seems to know them.

6. Make sure your children know exactly whom they may ride with. Either give them a list of these people, or devise a special password to be used by a person you send to pick them up. If your plans change unexpectedly and someone else must pick up your child for you, it is a very good idea to call your child's school or day-care center and tell them of the change and the name of the person who will be picking up your child. If possible inform your youngster directly of the change.

7. If you are concerned that a divorced spouse might try to abduct your children, make sure they know they should not go with that parent unless you've told them about the arrangements ahead of time. If a divorced spouse does not return the children home at the end of a visit, instruct them to phone you as soon as possible or get help from a trusted person or authority figure such as police officer, fire fighter, teacher, principal, doctor, nurse, or minister.

8. Confident children who know they're precious, valuable, and loved are much less apt to be abducted than insecure, ill-kempt youngsters with a low self-image. Abductors tend to prey upon children who are starved for attention, poorly dressed, and neglected because they know these young ones are often easy marks. According to convicted child abductors, children who are of slight build and are traveling alone in deserted areas or frequenting video arcades or convenience stores are prime targets for abduction. So are children between 8 and 10 who smoke cigarettes.

9. Review with your children what they should do if they are ever grabbed by a stranger. See page 190.

If You Think Your Child Has Been Abducted

First, remember that most youngsters who are thought to be missing turn up within hours. Children often wander off or go places without telling parents, and usually the incident ends happily. Most of the other youngsters classed as possible abductions are actually runaways who return home of their own volition. But if your child *is* missing, here's what you should do.

1. Phone your child's school, good friends, and casual friends to see if they know the youngster's whereabouts. Then phone your spouse, neighbors, and nearby relatives. Check all areas of your home, since the youngster may have simply crawled off for a nap.

2. If these efforts don't produce results within the hour, phone your local police department. Most police departments request that parents who think their child may have been kidnapped call them within an hour, or even sooner. Ask the police to file a report with the FBI, and if they hesitate, phone the FBI yourself with the information. If these agencies seem unresponsive, don't be afraid to be assertive and demanding; your child's life may be in danger.

3. Organize your own search party. Friends, relatives, and neighbors are good choices because they know and can recognize your child; other people will only have a description to go by. Local police may be able to suggest special groups who are often willing to help in such efforts. Search nearby areas, especially deserted places your youngster might frequent, abandoned refrigerators, packing boxes, even washers and dryers. If police do not conduct a house-to-house search, be sure to ask people in nearby homes if they have seen your child or noticed anything suspicious.

4. Always leave someone at home who knows the child well, in case the youngster returns. If your child finds no one home, he or she may leave again. Also make sure someone is there to answer the phone at all times.

5. If the search fails to turn up the missing child, contact organizations such as Child Find or Missing Children Help Center for support and suggestions. Your police department or telephone operator should have those phone numbers.

6. To protect yourself against crank calls or extortion, do not give your home phone number or address if you decide to give interviews or print posters of the missing child. Usually law enforcement agencies have phone numbers that can be used. Posters should show a recent, blown-up, full-face photograph of the child. List physical characteristics and the clothing your child was last seen wearing as well as any distinguishing features such as scars, birthmarks, or limps. Consider offering a reward for information leading to the return of your child; and if you decide to offer a reward, say that on the poster.

7. It is advisable to place ads, with your child's picture and description, in local, city, and out-of-town papers if you suspect the youngster was abducted by an ex-spouse.

8. Make it a practice to have a full-face photo of your child taken regularly so that you will always have a recent picture. On the back write the child's height and weight on the date the photo was taken. If you've had your child fingerprinted, keep the set of prints with this picture. You should also know where your child's dental x-rays are.

Abduction by a Spouse

Police report a dramatic increase in kidnappings by a parent because of divorce custody fights. Parents abduct their own children for various reasons. Often it's because they were not awarded custody and want the child with them. Or they see kidnapping as a way to hurt or get even with the other parent. If you are divorced and think your ex-spouse might try to abduct your child, take the following precautions.

1. Make sure your child's school, day-care center, and regular friends know that your child must not go with the other parent unless you have instructed them differently.

2. Tell your child never to go with the other parent unless you have told him in advance about the arrangements. If the other parent tries to force the child to come, instruct your youngster to resist, make a fuss, and try to get help.

3. Sometimes a vengeful spouse will tell the child that the custodial parent is angry and does not want him because of poor grades, trouble at home, or trouble with authorities. Make sure your child thoroughly understands that you will never be angry enough to give him up.

Activities for Practice

Phoning Collect

Have your kids make a collect call from your home phone and also from a pay phone so that they will know how to do this without adult help.

Bike Safety Check

Look over your children's bikes to make sure they are in safe riding condition. Correct any problems you find.

Home Bike Marathon

With chalk, draw an obstacle course on your driveway, a quiet street, or empty parking lot. See if your youngsters can "drive" their bikes safely through the course.

Being Followed

In various places in your neighborhood and town, have your kids imagine they are being followed, and ask where they would seek help. If your children walk to and from school, go along the way with them, and point out possible places where they could get help.

Getting a Description

Make a game out of teaching description skills. For instance, quietly point out a person, have your child study him, then later see how many things about the person your youngster can remember.

Getting the License Plate Number

When you're driving, see if your child can get the license plate number of an oncoming car and describe its make, model, and color. You can also play a game of memorizing license plate numbers. Have your child try to associate the letters and numbers with something important and see if that helps her remember. For instance, JRS might mean "Jumping Rope Safely" and 6239 could be associated with Grandma who is 62 and Dad who *says* he is 39!

What-If Games

"What would you do if" games help children consider beforehand how they would handle safety situations. This preplanning is invaluable when youngsters actually find themselves in a dangerous situation. Use the situations and information in this chapter as ideas for what-if games.

Role Playing

Role playing differs from what-if games because children can actually practice reacting when they role-play safety situations. When youngsters act out these plays, they are more apt to remember what they should do in a crisis situation. Try these role plays with your child.

MAN WITH THE MAP

The parent should play the part of a nicely dressed stranger, driving a new car. Pretend to pull the car up next to your youngster who is walking down the street. Show your child a map and ask for directions to a nearby location. See if your child remembers how he should respond.

SEE THE KITTENS

The parent should play the part of a stranger who drives his car up to your child who is walking home from school. Tell your child you have a box of kittens in the car and are going to have to have them put to sleep if you can't give them away. Ask your child to come look at them and suggest she could give one a good home. See if your child knows what the correct response should be.

LOST DOG

Have your child pretend he is playing in the park. The parent should take the role of a man asking for help finding his lost dog. Try to get your child to help you and suggest you both go into the nearby woods to search for the dog. If your child hesitates, offer him $10 to help.

NEWSPAPER PHOTOGRAPHER

The parent should play the part of a photographer with a local newspaper. Ask your child if you can take her picture for a special front-page feature story. Use flattery by mentioning you need a healthy-looking, beautiful child for a model, then ask the youngster to pose over in a wooded area, which would make a good backdrop for the picture. If your child hesitates, offer to send her an enlargement of the finished photograph and copies for all her relatives and teacher.

PAPERBOY

The parent should play the role of the paperboy. Offer your child some money if he will help you deliver papers. Tell him the papers are in your basement and he will have to go down with you to help carry them up. See how your child handles this situation.

AT THE BEACH

In this one, the parent should play the part of a woman who comes down to the beach and strikes up a conversation with your youngster. Talk about the nice weather and the fun the other children are having playing in the water with an old tire inner tube. Tell your youngster you have an inner tube in your car and will give it to her if she will come and get it.

PERSONALIZED SWEATSHIRT

Your child will have to pretend he is wearing a sweatshirt with his name printed on the back of it and he is waiting for a bus. The parent should play the role of a stranger who pulls his car up to the bus stop, calls out the youngster's name, says he knows the child's mom and dad, and offers to give him a ride home.

MAN WITH A BROKEN LEG

The parent should play the part of a man who has a cast on his leg. Go up to your child and ask her to help you carry several sacks of groceries up to your apartment. If the child hesitates tell her you have just gotten home from the hospital and feel weak and hungry. Try to shame your child by suggesting if she turns you down, she's deserting an old man with a handicap.

THE MAN AT SCHOOL

Here the parent should play the part of a man who comes up to your child while he is playing at the school grounds on a weekend. Tell your child you were supposed to meet your little girl there, but you can't find her. Ask your child to help you look around the deserted school buildings.

YOUR MOM'S BEEN HURT!

The parent should take the role of a stranger who comes up to your child and says her mother has been in an accident and has been rushed to the hospital. You, the stranger, are to take the child to see her mother. If your child hesitates, tell her, "Come on, there isn't much time. We have to get there right away.

Your mom told me to come get you. She wants to see you. We have to hurry before it's too late." See how your child handles this. It's helpful for youngsters to know that if a situation like this ever did occur, a hospital would almost always send a person known and trusted by the child, not a stranger.

DETOUR

In this play, the parent gets to pretend he's a young friend, or a sibling who tries to convince your child to take a new side trip on the way home from school. If your child resists, use peer pressure, such as calling him "Chicken," "Fraidy-cat," or "Momma's baby."

SHORTCUT

Again the parent should pretend to be a young brother or sister. Pretend you and your child are late getting home from a school play practice and you know your dad is going to be mad. Try to coax your child into taking a shortcut through a dark used-car lot because it will save a lot of time. If your child says no, accuse her of being a "scaredy-cat," afraid of the dark.

THE FORT IN THE WOODS

Pretend you are your child's friend and try to entice him to come with you to a log fort you have found in a deserted woods near your home. If your child refuses, see if he can come up with solutions that may preserve a friendship, yet keep you both safe.

HITCHHIKING

Pretend the two of you have walked 5 miles to the store; you're tired, and now it's raining. Suggest you both hitchhike home. If your child refuses, ask her for alternate suggestions.

YOUR RIDE IS DRUNK

Take the part of a neighborhood father who is going to give your child a ride home from baby-sitting. Act drunk and see if your child will accept the ride home or if he can successfully get out of riding with you.

ON THE BUS

The parent should pretend to be a stranger who sits down beside your child on the bus. Push up close to the youngster, ask her where she lives, and aggressively try to engage her in conversation. See if the child knows what to do.

MEAN DOG

Now the parent should pretend to be a mean dog who runs out and barks at your child when he is on his way home from school. See what your youngster will do.

GRABBED

The parent should pretend to be a stranger out to grab a child and pull him into some nearby bushes. When you do this activity, make sure your child understands this is only a pretend situation and she must be gentle in fighting you off!

NICE CAMERA

Take the part of a young "tough" who accosts your child on the street and tries to take his new camera. Call your child names and try to provoke him into fighting. Then, as a parent, give your child a big hug and remind him that even though you would both feel badly if his camera was stolen, his personal safety is more important to you than *any* camera in the whole wide world!

In Conclusion

It's a big and sometimes unsafe world we send our kids out into every day. We know there is always the chance of danger, but we also know that we can't wrap our kids in tissue paper and store them carefully on the top shelf out of harm's way! We *can't* isolate our kids from the world, but we *can* teach them how to avoid some of life's dangerous situations, cope with the threatening ones that do arise, and make decisions to keep themselves safe and sound when they are away from home.

Appendix

FORMS

IDENTIFICATION CARD

Name_____

Address_____

Home Phone Number_____

Mother's Name_____ Work Phone_____

Father's Name_____ Work Phone_____

Neighbors' Names and Phone Numbers

_____   _____

_____   _____

Doctor's Name and Phone Number

_____   _____

Dentist's Name and Phone Number

_____   _____

Important Medical Information_____

_____

IDENTIFICATION CARD

Name_____

Address_____

Home Phone Number_____

Mother's Name_____ Work Phone_____

Father's Name_____ Work Phone_____

Neighbors' Names and Phone Numbers

_____   _____

_____   _____

Doctor's Name and Phone Number

_____   _____

Dentist's Name and Phone Number

_____   _____

Important Medical Information_____

_____

IDENTIFICATION CARD

Name_____

Address_____

Home Phone Number_____

Mother's Name_____ Work Phone_____

Father's Name_____ Work Phone_____

Neighbors' Names and Phone Numbers

_____   _____

_____   _____

Doctor's Name and Phone Number

_____   _____

Dentist's Name and Phone Number

_____   _____

Important Medical Information_____

_____

IDENTIFICATION CARD

Name_____

Address_____

Home Phone Number_____

Mother's Name_____ Work Phone_____

Father's Name_____ Work Phone_____

Neighbors' Names and Phone Numbers

_____   _____

_____   _____

Doctor's Name and Phone Number

_____   _____

Dentist's Name and Phone Number

_____   _____

Important Medical Information_____

_____

EMERGENCY FORM: POST BY ALL PHONES

Police Department_____

Fire Department_____

Ambulance or Medic_____

Poison Center_____

Doctor_____

Dentist_____

Your Address_____

Nearest Cross Street_____

Mother at Work_____

Father at Work_____

Neighbors_____

_____

Other Information_____

_____

EMERGENCY FORM: POST BY ALL PHONES

Police Department_____

Fire Department_____

Ambulance or Medic_____

Poison Center_____

Doctor_____

Dentist_____

Your Address_____

Nearest Cross Street_____

Mother at Work_____

Father at Work_____

Neighbors_____

_____

Other Information_____

_____

CONSENT FOR MEDICAL CARE AND TREATMENT OF MINOR CHILDREN

Since hospitals are reluctant to treat children without consent of parents or guardians, delays may arise in treating a minor child who needs emergency care if parents or guardians are not readily available to give their consent. To avoid this delay, complete this two-page form. Leave one copy at home and one with neighbors.

I, _____, the natural parent/legal guardian of _____, authorize and consent to medical, surgical, and hospital care, treatment, and procedures to be performed for my child by a licensed physician or hospital when, in the sole discretion of the attending physician, such care, treatment, and procedures are immediately necessary or advisable in the interest of my child's health and well-being, and it is not advisable to take the time to contact me in advance.

Under the circumstances set forth above, I elect not to be informed in advance of the nature and character of the proposed treatment, its anticipated results, possible alternatives, and the risks, complications, and anticipated benefits involved in the proposed treatment and the alternative forms of treatment, including nontreatment.

Date_____
Signature of parent/guardian_____

Witness_____

INFORMATION ON THE CHILD

This form should accompany the consent form.

Child's name_____

Date of birth_____

Allergies and drug reactions_____

_____

Chronic illnesses_____

_____

Regular medications_____

_____

Other pertinent data_____

_____

Blood type _____ Date of last tetanus immunization_____

Child's physician _____ Phone_____

Parent's/guardian's address_____

Parent's/guardian's home phone number_____

Parent's/guardian's work phone number_____

Insurance coverage_____

Group number _____ Membership number_____

Employer_____